GT
Grand Touring

The World's Best GT Cars 1953 to 1973

Sam Dawson

Other great Veloce books!

SpeedPro Series
4-Cylinder Engine – How to Blueprint & Build a Short Block for High Performance (Hammill)
Alfa Romeo DOHC High-Performance Manual (Kartalamakis)
Alfa Romeo V6 Engine High-Perfomance Manual (Kartalamakis)
BMC 998cc A-Series Engine – How to Power Tune (Hammill)
1275cc A-Series High-Performance Manual (Hammill)
Camshafts – How to Choose & Time them for Maximum Power (Hammill)
Cylinder Heads – How to Build, Modify & Power Tune Updated & Revised Edition (Burgess & Gollan)
Distributor-type Ignition Systems – How to Build & Power Tune (Hammill)
Fast Road Car – How to Plan and Build Revised & Updated Colour New Edition (Stapleton)
Ford SOHC 'Pinto' & Sierra Cosworth DOHC Engines – How to Power Tune Updated & Enlarged Edition (Hammill)
Ford V8 – How to Power Tune Small Block Engines (Hammill)
Harley-Davidson Evolution Engines – How to Build & Power Tune (Hammill)
Holley Carburetors – How to Build & Power Tune Revised & Updated Edition (Hammill)
Jaguar XK Engines – How to Power Tune Revised & Updated Colour Edition (Hammill)
MG Midget & Austin-Healey Sprite – How to Power Tune Updated & Revised Edition (Stapleton)
MGB 4-Cylinder Engine – How to Power Tune (Burgess)
MGB V8 Power – How to Give Your Third, Colour Edition (Williams)
MGB, MGC & MGB V8 – How to Improve (Williams)
Mini Engines – How to Power Tune on a Small Budget Colour Edition (Hammill)
Motorsport – Getting Started (Collins)
Nitrous Oxide High-Performance Manual (Langfield)
Rover V8 Engines – How to Power Tune (Hammill)
Sportscar/Kitcar Suspension & Brakes – How to Build & Modify Enlarged & Updated 2nd Edition (Hammill)
SU Carburettor High-Performance Manual (Hammill)
Suzuki 4x4 – How to Modify for Serious Off-Road Action (Richardson)
Tiger Avon Sportscar – How to Build Your Own Updated & Revised 2nd Edition (Dudley)
TR2, 3 & TR4 – How to Improve (Williams)
TR5, 250 & TR6 – How to Improve (Williams)
TR7 & TR8, How to Improve (Williams)
V8 Engine – How to Build a Short Block for High Performance (Hammill)
Volkswagen Beetle Suspension, Brakes & Chassis – How to Modify for High Performance (Hale)
Volkswagen Bus Suspension, Brakes & Chassis – How to Modify for High Performance (Hale)
Weber DCOE, & Dellorto DHLA Carburetors – How to Build & Power Tune 3rd Edition (Hammill)

Those were the days ... Series
Alpine Trials & Rallies 1910-1973 (Pfundner)
Austerity Motoring (Bobbitt)
Brighton National Speed Trials (Gardiner)
British Police Cars (Walker)
Crystal Palace by (Collins)
Dune Buggy Phenomenon (Hale)
Dune Buggy Phenomenon Volume 2 (Hale)
MG's Abingdon Factory (Moylan)
Motor Racing at Brands Hatch in the Seventies (Parker)
Motor Racing at Goodwood in the Sixties (Gardiner)
Motor Racing at Oulton Park in the 60s (McFadyen)
Three Wheelers (Bobbitt)

Enthusiast's Restoration Manual Series
Citroën 2CV, How to Restore (Porter)
Classic Car Bodywork, How to Restore (Thaddeus)
Classic Car Electrics (Thaddeus)
Classic Cars, How to Paint (Thaddeus)
Reliant Regal, How to Restore (Payne)
Triumph TR2/3/3A, How to Restore (Williams)
Triumph TR4/4A, How to Restore (Williams)
Triumph TR5/250 & 6, How to Restore (Williams)
Triumph TR7/8, How to Restore (Williams)
Volkswagen Beetle, How to Restore (Tyler)
Yamaha FS1-E, How to Restore (Watts)

Essential Buyer's Guide Series
Alfa GT (Booker)
Alfa Romeo Spider Giulia (Booker)
Citroën 2CV (Paxton)
Jaguar E-type 3.8 & 4.2-litre (Crespin)
Jaguar E-type V12 5.3-litre (Crespin)
MGB & MGB GT (Williams)
Mercedes-Benz 280SL-560SL Roadsters (Bass)
Mercedes-Benz 'Pagoda' 230SL, 250SL & 280SL Roadsters & Coupés (Bass)
Morris Minor (Newell)
Porsche 928 (Hemmings)

Triumph TR6 (Williams)
VW Beetle (Cservenka & Copping)
VW Bus (Cservenka & Copping)

Auto-Graphics Series
Fiat-based Abarths (Sparrow)
Jaguar MkI & II Saloons (Sparrow)
Lambretta LI series scooters (Sparrow)

Rally Giants Series
Big Healey – 100-Six & 3000 (Robson)
Ford Escort MkI (Robson)
Lancia Stratos (Robson)
Peugeot 205 T16 (Robson)
Subaru Impreza (Robson)

General
1½-litre GP Racing 1961-1965 (Whitelock)
AC Two-litre Saloons & Buckland Sportscars (Archibald)
Alfa Romeo Giulia Coupé GT & GTA (Tipler)
Alfa Tipo 33 (McDonough & Collins)
Anatomy of the Works Minis (Moylan)
Armstrong-Siddeley (Smith)
Autodrome (Collins & Ireland)
Automotive A-Z, Lane's Dictionary of Automotive Terms (Lane)
Automotive Mascots (Kay & Springate)
Bahamas Speed Weeks, The (O'Neil)
Bentley Continental, Corniche and Azure (Bennett)
Bentley MkIV, Rolls-Royce Silver Wraith, Dawn & Cloud/Bentley R & S-series (Nutland)
BMC Competitions Department Secrets (Turner, Chambers & Browning)
BMW 5-Series (Cranswick)
BMW Z-Cars (Taylor)
British 250cc Racing Motorcycles by Chris Pereira
British Cars, The Complete Catalogue of, 1895-1975 (Culshaw & Horrobin)
BRM – a mechanic's tale (Salmon)
BRM V16 (Ludvigsen)
Bugatti Type 40 (Price)
Bugatti 46/50 Updated Edition (Price & Arbey)
Bugatti T44 & T49 (Price & Arbey)
Bugatti 57 2nd Edition (Price)
Caravans, The Illustrated History 1919-1959 (Jenkinson)
Caravans, The Illustrated History from 1960 (Jenkinson)
Chrysler 300 – America's Most Powerful Car 2nd Edition (Ackerson)
Chrysler PT Cruiser (Ackerson)
Citroën DS (Bobbitt)
Cobra – The Real Thing! (Legate)
Cortina – Ford's Bestseller (Robson)
Coventry Climax Racing Engines (Hammill)
Daimler SP250 'Dart' New Edition (Long)
Datsun Fairlady Roadster to 280ZX – The Z-car Story (Long)
Dino – The V6 Ferrari (Long)
Dodge Dynamite! (Grist)
Drive on the Wild Side – 20 extreme driving adventures from around the world, A (Weaver)
Ducati 750 Bible, The (Falloon)
Dune Buggy, Building a – The Essential Manual (Shakespeare)
Dune Buggy Files (Hale)
Dune Buggy Handbook (Hale)
Edward Turner: the man behind the motorcycles (Clew)
Fiat & Abarth 124 Spider & Coupé (Tipler)
Fiat & Abarth 500 & 600 2nd Edition (Bobbitt)
Fiats, Great Small (Ward)
Ford F100/F150 Pick-up 1948-1996 (Ackerson)
Ford F150 1997-2005 (Ackerson)
Ford GT – Then, and Now (Streather)
Ford GT40 (Legate)
Ford in Miniature (Olson)
Ford Model Y (Roberts)
Ford Thunderbird from 1954, The Book of the (Long)
Funky Mopeds (Skelton)
GT – The World's Best GT Cars 1953-73 (Dawson)
Hillclimbing & sprinting (Short)
Honda NSX (Long)
Jaguar, The Rise of (Price)
Jaguar XJ-S (Long)
Jeep CJ (Ackerson)
Jeep Wrangler (Ackerson)
Karmann-Ghia Coupé & Convertible (Bobbitt)
Lambretta Bible, The (Davies)
Lancia Delta HF Integrale (Blaettel & Wagner)
Land Rover, The Half-Ton Military (Cook)
Laverda Twins & Triples Bible 1968-1986 (Falloon)
Lea-Francis Story, The (Price)
Lexus Story, The (Long)
Lola – The Illustrated History (1957-1977) (Starkey)

Lola – All the Sports Racing & Single-Seater Racing Cars 1978-1997 (Starkey)
Lola T70 – The Racing History & Individual Chassis Record 3rd Edition (Starkey)
Lotus 49 (Oliver)
MarketingMobiles, The Wonderful Wacky World of (Hale)
Mazda MX-5/Miata 1.6 Enthusiast's Workshop Manual (Grainger & Shoemark)
Mazda MX-5/Miata 1.8 Enthusiast's Workshop Manual (Grainger & Shoemark)
Mazda MX-5 Miata: the book of the world's favourite sportscar (Long)
Mazda MX-5 Miata Roadster (Long)
MGA (Price Williams)
MGB & MGB GT – Expert Guide (Auto-Doc Series) (Williams)
MGB Electrical Systems (Astley)
Micro Caravans (Jenkinson)
Microcars at large! (Quellin)
Mini Cooper – The Real Thing! (Tipler)
Mitsubishi Lancer Evo, the road car & WRC story (Long)
Montlhéry, the story of the Paris autodrome (Boddy)
Moto Guzzi Sport & Le Mans Bible (Falloon)
Motor Movies – The Posters! (Veysey)
Motor Racing – Reflections of a Lost Era (Carter)
Motorcycle Road & Racing Chassis Designs (Knoakes)
Motorhomes, The Illustrated History (Jenkinson)
Motorsport in colour, 1950s (Wainwright)
Nissan 300ZX & 350Z – The Z-Car Story (Long)
Pass the Theory and Practical Driving Tests (Gibson & Hoole)
Pontiac Firebird (Cranswick)
Porsche Boxster (Long)
Porsche 356 (Long)
Porsche 911 Carrera – The Last of the Evolution (Corlett)
Porsche 911R, RS & RSR, 4th Edition (Starkey)
Porsche 911 – The Definitive History 1963-1971 (Long)
Porsche 911 – The Definitive History 1971-1977 (Long)
Porsche 911 – The Definitive History 1977-1987 (Long)
Porsche 911 – The Definitive History 1987-1997 (Long)
Porsche 911 – The Definitive History 1997-2004 (Long)
Porsche 911SC 'Super Carrera' – The Essential Companion (Streather)
Porsche 914 & 914-6: The Definitive History Of The Road & Competition Cars (Long)
Porsche 924 (Long)
Porsche 944 (Long)
Porsche 993 'King of Porsche' – The Essential Companion (Streather)
Porsche Racing Cars – 1953 to 1975 (Long)
Porsche Racing Cars – 1976 on (Long)
Porsche – The Rally Story (Meredith)
Porsche: Three Generations of Genius (Meredith)
RAC Rally Action! (Gardiner)
Rallye Sport Fords: the inside story (Moreton)
Redman, Jim – 6 Times World Motorcycle Champion: The Autobiography (Redman)
Rolls-Royce Silver Shadow/Bentley T Series Corniche & Camargue Revised & Enlarged Edition (Bobbitt)
Rolls-Royce Silver Spirit, Silver Spur & Bentley Mulsanne 2nd Edition (Bobbitt)
RX-7 – Mazda's Rotary Engine Sportscar (updated & revised new edition) (Long)
Scooters & Microcars, The A-Z of popular (Dan)
Singer Story: Cars, Commercial Vehicles, Bicycles & Motorcycles (Atkinson)
SM – Citroën's Maserati-engined Supercar (Long & Claverol)
Subaru Impreza: the road car and WRC story (Long)
Taxi! The Story of the 'London' Taxicab (Bobbitt)
Toyota Celica & Supra (Long)
Toyota MR2 Coupés & Spyders (Long)
Triumph Motorcycles & the Meriden Factory (Hancox)
Triumph Speed Twin & Thunderbird Bible (Woolridge)
Triumph Tiger Cub Bible (Estall)
Triumph Trophy Bible (Woolridge)
Triumph TR6 (Kimberley)
Unraced (Collins)
Velocette Motorcycles – MSS to Thruxton Updated & Revised (Burris)
Virgil Exner – Visioneer: The official biography of Virgil M Exner designer extraordinaire (Grist)
Volkswagen Bus Book, The (Bobbitt)
Volkswagen Bus or Van to Camper, How to Convert (Porter)
Volkswagens of the World (Glen)
VW Beetle Cabriolet (Bobbitt)
VW Beetle – The Car of the 20th Century (Copping)
VW Bus – 40 years of Splitties, Bays & Wedges (Copping)
VW Bus Book, The (Bobbitt)
VW Golf: five generations of fun (Copping & Cservenka)
VW – The air-cooled era (Copping)
VW T5 Camper Conversion Manual (Porter)
VW Campers (Copping)
Works Minis, The Last (Purves & Brenchley)
Works Rally Mechanic (Moylan)

www.veloce.co.uk

First published in March 2007 by Veloce Publishing Limited, 33 Trinity Street, Dorchester DT1 1TT, England. Fax 01305 268864/e-mail info@veloce.co.uk/web www.veloce.co.uk or www.velocebooks.com.
ISBN: 978-1-84584-060-0/UPC: 636847-04060-4

GT

Grand Touring

The World's Best GT Cars 1953 to 1973

Sam Dawson

VELOCE

Contents

Introduction. 6

Acknowledgements 9

1953-63: extravagance emerges from the shadow of war 10

Lancia Aurelia B20 GT 12

Bristol 401-406.. 14

Bentley Continental/S-series Continental 16

Aston Martin DB 2/4 MkI, II & III.. 18

Jaguar XK140 & XK150 fhc.. 20

Facel Vega FVS/HK500.. 22

Jensen 541 24

BMW 503. 26

Alvis TD21 28

Alfa Romeo Giulietta SS & Giulia SS 30

Aston Martin DB4. 33

Maserati 3500GT/GTI. 35

AC Greyhound 37

Lancia Flaminia Coupé/GT 39

Ferrari 250GTE, GTB Lusso and 330 America. 41

1963-73: power meets the motorway age. 43

Volvo P1800, 1800E, 1800S & 1800ES.. 45

FIAT 2300S & Dino Coupé.. 47

Jaguar XKE ('E-type') 49

Facel Vega Facel II 51

Alfa Romeo 2600 Sprint 53

Bentley S3 & T1 Coupés, Rolls-Royce Silver Shadow Coupé & Corniche.. 55

Iso Rivolta, Grifo & Lele 58

Bristol 407, 408, 409, 410 and 411 series 1-5 … … … … … … … … … … … … … 61

Jensen CV8 & Interceptor … … … … … … … … … … … … … … … … … … … 64

Alfa Romeo Giulia Sprint GT, GT Junior and GTV … … … … … … … … … … … 67

Alvis TE21 & TF21 … 69

Aston Martin DB5, DB6, DBS & AM Vantage … … … … … … … … … … … … … 71

Buick Riviera … 74

Maserati Sebring & Mistral … … … … … … … … … … … … … … … … … … 76

Maserati Mexico & Indy … … … … … … … … … … … … … … … … … … … 79

Studebaker Avanti, Avanti II & AAC Avanti … … … … … … … … … … … … … 82

Gordon-Keeble GK1 … 85

Reliant Scimitar … 87

Ferrari 330GT 2+2, 330GTC & 365GTC … … … … … … … … … … … … … … 89

Oldsmobile Toronado … … … … … … … … … … … … … … … … … … … 91

BMW CS … 93

Lamborghini 400GT & Islero … … … … … … … … … … … … … … … … … 96

Mazda 110S Cosmo … 98

Gilbern Genie & Invader … … … … … … … … … … … … … … … … … … 100

Jensen FF … 102

AC 428 … 104

Lotus Elan +2 … 106

Ferrari 365GT 2+2 & GTC/4 … … … … … … … … … … … … … … … … … 108

Mercedes-Benz CE/SE … … … … … … … … … … … … … … … … … … … 111

Lamborghini Espada & Jarama … … … … … … … … … … … … … … … … 114

Reliant Scimitar GTE & GTC … … … … … … … … … … … … … … … … … 117

Aston Martin DBS V8, DBSS, V8, Vantage, Volante & Zagato … … … … … … … 120

Lancia Flavia 2000 Coupé … … … … … … … … … … … … … … … … … … 124

Marcos Mantis … 126

Citroën SM … 128

Triumph Stag … 130

FIAT 130 Coupé … 132

Bitter CD … 134

1973 – the end of an era … … … … … … … … … … … … … … … … … … 136

Index … 142

GT: 50 years of getting there in style

Introduction

Of all the terms in the motoring lexicon, the 'GT' moniker has to be one of the most misused and abused. Even today, a casual glance at the new cars on sale will reveal a miscellany of hot hatches, urbane two-door saloons, family cars loaded with extras, top-end engines and sullying body-kits, all wearing the 'GT' badge. Nowadays, and indeed for many years, 'GT' has merely been a specification. It has been misrepresented at the other end of the scale too. To many motorsport fans, a GT car is a racing supercar – fast, raw, endowed with a massive engine, headline-making performance statistics and almost zero on-road credentials, in short, a track-bound racer. But it is so much more than that: GT – Grand Tourer, Gran Turismo, or the French version: Grande Routière – whatever language it speaks, is far from being a box to tick on an options list. GT cars are still being built, some have never gone away. The ideal of a car with the ability to cross a continent at speed and in comfort yet provide driving thrills when demanded has always found favour with a clique of owners which will insist on being called 'motorists' rather than merely 'drivers'. But this exclusivity is not based around price. True, many GT cars have enormous price tags and tiny production runs, but as will be demonstrated, many of the best, most revolutionary and groundbreaking Grand Tourers have been found in 'real world' price lists, sold by mass-manufacturers alongside more prosaic saloons.

So what makes a true GT? I have set down criteria to filter out the pretenders, the compromisers and the over-compensators to avoid this book running into biblical proportions.

1   A GT car must have been created from the start as a GT car. A two-door saloon, for example the BMW 02, with its profusion of body styles and engines, cannot be regarded as a car created for grand touring. Dedicated coupés using the touring ability of top-end saloon parts, however, such as the Lancia Aurelia B20 GT, have been included as their conception was clearly separate from the rest of the range.

2   A GT is capable of grand touring in all its guises as part of the purity of its conception. If the Volkswagen Scirocco can be regarded as having GT abilities in 110bhp Storm GLI form,

but not in 50bhp 1100 guise, then its conception as a GT car is compromised and it cannot be regarded as such. However, a car using top-end components from the range in a dedicated GT car, for example the Volvo P1800, can be seen as such, due to the intentions of its creation.

THE FACT THAT THE GT DREAM HAS REMAINED ALIVE THROUGH TIMES OF AUSTERITY AND RECESSION, THROUGH RUTHLESS EXPANSION, OIL CRISES, TECHNOLOGY, OVER-REGULATION AND THE FORCES OF FASHION SHOWS THAT THE SPECIES CAN ADAPT AND SURVIVE WHEN SO MANY CONTEMPORARIES FALL FROM GRACE.

3   Supercars are not, by default, GT cars. This does not prevent a GT, or a version of such, from being a supercar – the Aston Martin Vantage Zagato's record-breaking power output, for example, makes it a supercar, but its original intention was as a GT. However, the majority of cars constructed to do 200mph plus, or accelerate to sixty in under four seconds lack both the relaxing refinement and inherent practicality that a sister GT model manages. As a result, the Ferrari 365GTB/4 'Daytona' is not included among the GTs in this book, but its more refined, four-seater related cousins, the 365GT 2+2 and C/4, however, are.

4   Neither, for that matter, is a sports coupé automatically a GT. It may be argued that such cars as the Chevrolet Camaro, Triumph GT6 and Bond Equipe are coupés with luggage space

Opposite: Typical of the grand touring breed is the Lamborghini 400GT – a 2+2 seating configuration, a large, powerful engine, a degree of racing thinking adapted for the road, and a definite usability. (Courtesy David Hodges Collection)

and fun performance, but their underpinnings are too firm and their engines too harsh to enter the GT class. This is not to say that a sports car with the potential for refinement cannot lay the groundwork for a GT car. For example, the Jaguar XK120 evolved into the more practical and useable XK140.

5   For the sake of the refinement argument, cars conceived from the off as convertibles cannot be automatically considered GTs either. This does not prevent, of course, a GT car having a convertible version available alongside the coupé (the 'Volante' versions of most Aston Martins spring to mind), but removing the roof also removes the car's usefulness in all weathers – necessary when crossing continents. It also removes the possibility of the added practicality of a hatchback and associated usable luggage space, as found on such GTs as the Aston Martin DB2/4 and Jaguar E-type Coupé, but not on a DB2 Drophead or E-type Roadster.

6   Ideally, the GT car should have been devised by its progenitors as a Grand Tourer, with all associated considerations in mind. It should be able to transport at least two in comfort with their luggage and have space to spare – probably in the form of a two plus two (2+2) seating arrangement. All the engines fitted should be able to cope with cruising comfortably at the upper limits on all continental roads without drawbacks or loss of usable power. The design of the car, inside and out, should be geared towards its complete control by the driver; and the chassis and suspension should also provide suitable handling and roadholding on all routes that might be encountered on one's travels (were it not for its perimeter-frame chassis and soggy suspension, the Cadillac Eldorado would doubtlessly have made it into this book).

I have begun this celebration of the GT car in 1953 for a

Grand tourers must possess a degree of practicality. Most of the cars in this book (such as this Espada) possess large luggage compartments and at least 2+2 seating. (Courtesy David Hodges Collection)

variety of reasons. Firstly, despite its potential to fill many sumptuous volumes, the history of the GT car prior to the Second World War was rooted largely in a tradition of separate chassis, engines and coachbuilders. If a car buyer in the 1920s and 1930s wanted a GT car, he or she would have to commission a variety of manufacturers and the result would be highly individual, often clothed in a work of Art Deco splendour, but there would be nothing to separate the concept of the GT from a completely different type of car using the same essential 'ingredients'. For example, the six Bugatti Royales built encompass Grand Tourers, limousines and sports cars. The modern GT is one built under expert eyes using a cocktail of professionally selected methods and components, the first being the Lancia Aurelia B20 GT.

Also, prior to the 1950s, there were few roads on which to take your GT. With the exception of town roads (hardly the environment for such a car), many routes were along rugged tracks. As the first arterial road appeared after the war, the ability to link them together and travel at speed for long distances bore fruit in the GT car. Peacetime lifted the boundary restrictions in Europe, and the lure of taking a long trip abroad under your own steam, carrying your own luggage to exotic destinations held as much appeal as it does today.

The grand touring story is, in many ways, one of survival. The fact that the GT dream has remained alive through times of austerity and recession, through ruthless expansion, oil crises, technology, over-regulation and the forces of fashion shows that the species can adapt and survive when so many contemporaries fall from grace. As a concept, grand touring (unlike the raw, unassisted hot-hatch of the '80s, or the excessive American land yacht of the '50s) has remained unadulterated, mature, and very much alive.

So pack a battered old leather suitcase, slip into something comfortable, and enjoy this winding route through the great ages of the long-distance sports tourer. Be inspired!

Acknowledgements

This book is dedicated to the old boys and girls of the York University Karting Club (YUKC), who always knew I'd end up doing something like this.

For their invaluable help in sourcing photographs, cars and information, thanks must go (in no particular order) to:

Richard MacArthur, Martin Brewer, Stuart Pugh, the Alfa Romeo Owners' Club, Charles and Ed Herridge, Roy and Patricia Dowding, Paul Abadjian, Martin J Daly, the Ferrari Owners' Club GB, Rick Clough, Karl Eric Malberg, the Swedish Volvo P1800 Owners' Club, Peter Jones, the FIAT Club UK, Dani Latuskie, PistonHeads, Chris Harper, Mark Collins, M R De Vries, Chris Knowles, the Buick Riviera Owners' Club (US), S Childs, EMAP Automotive Archive, Tony Turner, Jacqueline Harris, Justin Wells, the Gordon-Keeble Owners' Club, John Simpson, Scimitar Owners' Club, Kris Trexler, Oldsmobile Toronado Owners' Club (US), David Poole, John Webster and the Marcos Owners' Club.

... and, for their advice, support and error-correcting, to:

BMW Owners' Club UK, Andreas Klugschied, BMW Pressgruppe, the AC Owners' Club GB, SeMantics Citroën SM Club, Diana Housego-Woolgar, the Facel Vega Owners' Club, Max Weitzmann, Mark Hughes, and, most importantly, Rod Grainger.

Below is a selected list of prestige dealerships, where many of the grand touring cars found in this book are often on sale:

In the UK:
Runnymede Motor Company (specialists in classic Aston Martins)
Web: www.runnymedemotorcompany.com
Email: sales@runnymedemotorcompany.com
Tel: 01753 644599/07836 222111

The School Garage (specialists in classic British and European cars)
Web: www.classiccarshop.co.uk
Tel: 01663 733209/07767 617507

Retro Classics Ltd (specialists in classic Jaguar)
Web: www.retroclassics.com
Email: mail@retroclassics.com
Tel: 0207 937 1206

Justin Banks Classic Cars (specialist in interesting classic cars)
Web: www.justinbanks.com

In the USA:
Bob's Classics (specialists in European and American rarities, including Avanti)
Web: www.bobsclassics.com

1953-63: extravagance emerges from the shadow of war

The 1950s were, in many ways, an embryonic time for the national motoring characteristics that would influence the GT car. Initially a curiously European concoction, the GT was among the first non-utility products to emerge from previously war-ravaged economies after more than ten years of recession and crippling debt.

Releasing a GT car at this time was a hit-and-miss business. Prior to 1953, petrol rationing had stifled the market, and economic restart policies had put paid to many image-building, loss-leading GT cars that, had they emerged just a few years later, could possibly have been a success. The British Invicta Black Prince and the French Rosengart Supertrahuit spring to mind as GTs that 'might have been' were it not for a non-existent market in the late 1940s. The Americans, even in their optimistic internationalist phase, politically-speaking, of the 1950s, had yet to cotton on to the ethos of the GT car, preferring to build machines more suited to their long, straight, smooth roads and labour-saving lifestyles, despite the fact that they formed the largest market for European GT cars, a fact that holds true to this day. The Japanese automotive industry, on the other hand, was still licence-building Austin Sevens in ruined post-war surroundings, with no sign of the rampant industrialisation and vibrant innovation that would come to characterise Japanese cars in later years.

The GT cars of the 1950s in many ways suggested a continuation and refinement of previous designs. Britain dominated the period numerically, the GTs characterised almost by default by their straight-six engines of three to four litres and bodywork suggestive of smoothed-off pre-war coachbuilt cars. Yet British design was also trendsetting. The low-cost, high-speed and dramatic Jaguar XK series replaced the MG T-series as the image of a perfect British sports car, refined to GT status by the later 140 and 150 models and a bestseller in America. Bentley began – albeit subtly – the trend for American-inspired design on smaller British cars, influenced as it was by contemporary Cadillacs, yet with typically European restraint and an emphasis on an invigorating drive.

If Britain can be seen as the most predictable manufacturer in this period, then Italy was the most diverse. Although Lancia and Maserati followed the British recipe for the most part, the new-age Superleggera bodywork techniques and

FERRARI ALSO MADE IN-ROADS INTO THE GT MARKET, KICKING OFF A DYNASTY OF WONDERFULLY REFINED DRIVER'S GTs THAT CONTINUES AS STRONG AS EVER TODAY.

Touring Milano styling would go on to influence many of the world's greatest GT cars, most notably the Aston Martin DB4 of 1958. Alfa Romeo, with its Giulia SS, experimented with the benefits of aerodynamics to produce a combination of a relatively small engine, light weight and high speed – a blend that would achieve huge desirability during the 1970s oil crisis. Ferrari also made in-roads into the GT market, after refining its previously crude, albeit stunningly fast, V12 racing cars into the magnificent 250GTE, kicking off a dynasty of wonderfully refined driver's GTs that continues as strong as ever today with the 612 Scaglietti homage.

The 1950s must also be remembered as a somewhat bittersweet time for the GT car. Due to less than advantageous financial conditions, all GTs were expensive both to build and buy, making it a highly exclusive breed that required success to stay alive. Many ambitious yet obscure projects fell by the wayside through lack of money. Panhard's CD and 24CT, although advanced in so many areas, lacked the power and refinement to be a true GT, and British firms such as Lotus and TVR were chasing volume sales and track success through the quintessentially British kit specials market.

Yet the '50s produced so many of the innovations that went on to define the GT car for future generations. Pioneers used aerodynamics, wind tunnels, weight saving measures and large, stock-specification American V8s in sophisticated European cars in a decade that laid the groundwork for the golden age of the GT car.

Many upmarket early fifties GT cars still clung to the pre-war coachbuilt formula, like this Bentley R-Type Continental. (Courtesy David Hodges Collection)

The fifties were a time of tentative experimentation with weight reduction and aerodynamics by coachbuilders such as Zagato. (Courtesy Stuart Pugh)

Lancia Aurelia B20 GT

Generally regarded by experts as the first true GT car, the Lancia Aurelia B20 GT certainly laid down the template for the European model of cross-continental sophistication, and was the first car to be generally termed a 'GT'. That it could be used on a long tour and could still be taken, very effectively, to the track also set it years ahead of its time in terms of ability. The fact that, in 1950, it was not the most expensive or exclusive car to do so also makes the fact that it is so revered today (price-wise especially) unsurprising.

Following a practise many other manufacturers would take to heart, Lancia shortened the chassis of its Aurelia B10 saloon to produce the basis for the B20 GT. Initially sporting the 2-litre V6, standard in the B10 saloon, the Lancia revved smoothly throughout its range and held the road like a racer. Despite being slightly austere inside and featuring a most unsporting column change (all hangovers from the saloon), the sporting intent was not lost on the Grand Prix champions of the 1950s – both Argentina's Juan Manuel Fangio and England's Mike Hawthorne found the Lancia's character invigorating and relaxing alongside their Formula 1 mounts from the likes of Maserati and Ferrari.

GRACEFUL AND UNADORNED, ITS SUBTLETY MARKED IT OUT DRAMATICALLY FROM OTHER SHORT-LIVED AND WAYWARD FASHIONS OF THE 1950s.

Recognising the weakness of the gearbox in this sporting concoction, Nardi offered a four-speed, floor-mounted conversion. These were perhaps the best of the early Aurelias, as the engine was tweaked slightly to suit the new gearbox, which could make lighter work of the engine, now producing somewhat more than the standard 112bhp. Prince Ranier of Monaco was a Nardi conversion customer. Not to say the standard engine itself was in any way backwards. Lancia had the first 'production' V6 to its name, and the Aurelia's V6 built upon that, with its American-inspired hemi-style combustion chambers and double-choke carburettor. Light alloy components made up

a lightweight engine that, balanced with the gearbox, made for an almost perfect weight distribution typical of sporting Italian cars.

SPECIFICATION
CYLINDERS = V6
CAPACITY (LITRES) = 2.0-2.5
POWER = 112BHP
TOP SPEED = 112MPH
TRANSMISSION = 4-SPEED MANUAL
DESIGN = VITTORIO JANO, PININFARINA
BUILT = 1950-58

The march of time forced changes, but none as radical on this advanced GT car. Small details such as the deletion of window quarter-lights, improved light clusters and increased luxury options inside the car were natural. However, the series 4 cars from 1954 (Aurelia B20 GTs went through six 'series' upgrades between 1950 and 1958) featured imported DeDion rear suspension which solved the tail-happy nature of the in-house Lancia trailing-arm system, later adopted across the range, as well as an engine bore-out – 2.4 litres now made the Aurelia more competitive in an expanding market.

One thing that could not change, though, was the styling. Graceful and unadorned, its subtlety marked it out dramatically from other short-lived and wayward fashions of the 1950s. During its run, various coachbuilders, such as Zagato and Vignale, attempted to impose other styles on it to varying success, but not one seemed to match Jano's original vision of the perfect grand touring car. Viewing it today reveals the wealth of designs it inspired; from the likes of Porsche (side profile of the 911), Aston Martin (rear end on the DB2/4) and Daimler (front end of the Majestic).

All in all, the high prices of today's market only reflect the revelation that the Aurelia B20 GT was. Always expensive, the choice of some of the greatest Formula 1 champions will always be worth the asking price.

Favoured transport of many professional competition drivers when new, the Lancia Aurelia B20 GT proved itself equally adept in both luxury and sporting usage. (Courtesy David Hodges Collection)

Bristol 401-406

In many ways, Bristol's 400-series was one of the most advanced GT cars of the '50s, and in some respects was a precursor of the more aerodynamically focused, lightweight GTs of later years. Had it not been for the influence of the likes of Facel-Vega throughout the GT world, it is possible that Bristol would still be producing lithe, aerodynamic and economical cars, rather than the big-block Chrysler-powered throwbacks the company is famous for today.

Yet in many respects the 400-series has more in common with German engineering than British. The autobahn-exploiting 2-litre engine was originally a BMW unit, acquired as part of post-war reparations agreements, and few would argue against the similarity of the aerodynamic body, complete with a BMW 'kidney grille', to the German cars that originally bore the engine. In construction, though, the Bristol was traditional, what with its separate chassis, although in an era when monocoques were still associated with noisy, firm-riding sports cars, this is hardly surprising.

Bristol has always taken pride in its aircraft-building credentials. The glamour of air travel, coupled with the retained spirit of wartime air power always found favour with what would be later termed 'the jet set'. Ownership glitterati included period performers Jean Simmons and Stewart Granger. Bristol, of course, never let the aircraft connection remain simply a question of image – the

400-series was the first car to be designed with the aid of a wind tunnel, and the aircraft-specification alloy bodyshell, whilst being incredibly strong, featured varying thickness depending on the load-bearing properties – e.g. around opening apertures and the tops of the wings where mechanics might lean – thinking taken directly from the need for an aircraft to be simultaneously lightweight and load bearing in parts.

All these advances made for not only a reliable and luxurious car, capable of silent high-speed cruising in the Bentley league, but also an economical one, the construction techniques allowing for

The styling of the early post-war Bristol Grand Tourers made no attempt to hide their BMW origins, even though it had evolved in the wind tunnel. (Courtesy David Hodges Collection)

miles per gallon figures in excess of 25, excellent when compared to all rivals. Further aerodynamic experimentation urged greater performance from the later model, the finned, two-seater 404.

Of course, laying down such a challenge led to a raft of rivals appearing as the economic climate improved in the early 1950s, and the sheer grunt of less sophisticated rivals from the likes of Alvis and Aston Martin began to make the Bristol look increasingly underpowered. A bore-out to 2.2-litres, coupled with a new, more 'current' looking coupé bodyshell derived from the looks of the 404 and 405 four-door saloon made the Bristol 406 more of

SPECIFICATION
CYLINDERS = 6
CAPACITY (LITRES) = 2.0-2.2
POWER = 85-130BHP
TOP SPEED = 97-105MPH
TRANSMISSION = 4-SPEED MANUAL OVERDRIVE
DESIGN = BRISTOL IN-HOUSE/GIANNI ZAGATO, ZAGATO
BUILT = 1948-61

a contender. As a result it lasted from 1953 to 1961, when it became clear that the immediate future of the GT market lay in greater horsepower and displacements.

The story of the Bristol 406 does not end there, however. In 1959, Bristol dealer and current manager Tony Crook recognised the finite appeal of the ageing 406, and saw a future for it in the work of Italian coachbuilder Zagato. Gianni Zagato designed a beautiful bodyshell not dissimilar to period Lancias, boasting a lighter weight and greater aerodynamic coefficient than the standard 406. Unfortunately, due to high pricing and the limited appeal of what was essentially a pre-war engine, Crook only managed to commission six 406Zs for customers, but as a classic car, it is the most valued of the landmark Bristol 400-series.

Although conceived as a long-distance tourer, the Bristol 400 series acquitted itself well as a rally car – an ability still demonstrated in revival events today. (Courtesy David Hodges Collection)

Bentley Continental/S-series Continental

Bentley's iconic Continental simultaneously marks both the end of an archaic era of GT building and the dramatic beginning of another. The story of the Continental, once the very pinnacle of the British interpretation of grand touring, is also an unfortunate one of stagnation and loss of identity under the ownership of Rolls-Royce.

The Continental name was perfectly apt, not only due to its seamless ability to traverse a continent in speed and comfort, but also the nature of its sale: due to crippling purchase tax in Britain, it was originally offered as an export only. Intended to restore Bentley's increasingly patrician image of the ageing MkVI sports saloon, with its separate running boards and pre-war construction techniques, the Continental was revealed to a stunned audience in 1952, with austerity still firmly in its mind.

It also began a trend in British car design that few would admit to at the time for reasons of pride: the influence of American design. The classic Cadillac Series 62 Coupe lent its sublime sloping fastback, billowing wings and subtle fins to John Blatchley's design, beginning a fad for copying and downsizing American design throughout the 1950s on everything from the humble Nash-inspired Standard Vanguard to the glitzy Cadillac Eldorado Biarritz-aping Vauxhall Cresta. It no doubt helped sales in America too, becoming a favourite of A-list movie stars and establishment industrialists across the Atlantic. Famous Brits able to purchase one outside the country were drawn to its suave appeal: Ian Fleming, living in Jamaica, drove one, appropriately portraying James Bond behind the wheel of one in his classic novel *Thunderball*. It soon gained a reputation for reliability to match its solid image, galvanized by the proud grille still distantly associated with the Le Mans challengers of the 1920s.

What was most definitely un-American was the way it drove. With the recommended manual transmission and safe traction, coupled with an aluminium body for lighter weight,

Interiors became more opulent during the car's production life. This is a later model with large leather seats in place of the original's cloth-upholstered sports items.
(Courtesy Martin Brewer)

SPECIFICATION
CYLINDERS = 6/V8
CAPACITY (LITRES) = 4.6-6.2
POWER = 200BHP (EST.)
TOP SPEED = 106-124MPH
TRANSMISSION = 4-SPEED MANUAL/4-SPEED AUTOMATIC
DESIGN = JOHN BLATCHLEY, H J MULLINER
BUILT = 1952-59

it rewarded keen drivers and cemented the image of the British GT in the minds of wealthy foreign customers in a way the very much home-bound Bristol 400-series had not. Even the touring fuel consumption was favourable on longer journeys – up to 24 miles per gallon – proving the benefits of its thoroughly modern design.

But it was not to last. Ironically a victim of its own success, its neat hip-hugging cloth-lined seats were replaced with wide leather armchairs, along with an engine bore-out from 4.6 to 4.9 litres, all due to customer demand. Automatics became more prevalent, and it became obvious to Rolls-Royce that the meticulous way they were coach-built could not be continued to match demand. In 1955, the Bentley Continental S1 appeared, a touring coupé contraction of the new Rolls-Royce Silver Cloud, with a large and thirsty American-inspired 6.2-litre V8 and only a grille and badges to set it apart.

After four years of production, the light-bodied S1 was replaced by the heavy, 'Standard Steel'-bodied S2.

The fastback design of the Bentley R-Type Continental, attributed to John Blatchley and built by H J Mulliner, was stongly influenced by contemporary Cadillacs. (Courtesy David Hodges Collection)

Rolls-Royce ditched the manual transmission option and blunted its sprightliness with further Silver Cloud-derived luxury fittings. Although highly successful, its ubiquity keeps the prices out of the range of the original Continental, a car it struggled to match in terms of commensurate driving ability, although its reputation for quality and style can never be faulted.

Aston Martin DB 2/4 MkI, II & III

Despite its current enviable reputation for producing some of the finest and most capable cars of the GT genre, Aston Martin's roots are in much more Spartan cars. Although the engines were highly advanced, Aston Martin's pre-war reputation was founded on starkly successful race-winners with small four-cylinder engines. Although capacities and cylinder numbers increased, the competition bent carried over very much to its first post-war road cars, the DB1 and DB2.

Perhaps it was the influence of its more luxury-orientated sister company, Lagonda, that prompted Aston Martin to 'evolve' the cramped and raucous DB2 sports car (that ran, almost in standard form, at Le Mans) into the grand touring DB2/4 series. Aston Martin already used the Lagonda LB6 engine, designed by Willie Watson to rival the Jaguar XK six and originally installed in a Lagonda saloon as well as the DB2. Bored out to 3 litres for greater smoothness and long-distance refinement, this improved engine found its way into the DB2/4.

The refinement was not in any way restricted to the engine bay. The DB2 chassis was stretched 7in and two small seats were installed in the rear (hence the '/4'). Competition practise dictated a larger fuel tank for touring use, and the chassis stretch allowed for a boot capacious enough for a reasonable amount of luggage. Changes to the rear design of the DB2 included, most notably, a more sweeping tail with an oval-shaped, side-hinged hatchback which doubtlessly inspired the Jaguar E-type coupé's rear lines nearly ten years later. The interior, setting the standard for future Aston Martins, was swaddled in high quality leather and thicker-piled carpets. Improving the soundproofing made for a more relaxed touring experience.

After 565 cars built, Aston Martin's purchase of the Tickford coachbuilders for the manufacture of Lagondas made for a more practical proposition than farming the contract out to H J Mulliner. With the switch to Tickford came some revisions to the car design, dubbed DB 2/4 MkII, that pointed the way forward to future Aston Martins: The curvaceous rear sprouted subtle finned plinths for the rear lights, and a bold chrome strake appeared on the new, higher bonnet shut-line, where a similarly straked air duct would appear on every Aston Martin from the 1958 DB4 onwards. The chrome lining around the glasshouse was criticised for its lack of taste at the time, although the rarity of these cars (199 built) makes them the most sought after today, and in a world of gruesome plastic bodykits, the chromed lines are positively classy.

SPECIFICATION
Cylinders = 6
Capacity (litres) = 3.0
Power = 140-162BHP
Top speed = 117MPH
Transmission = 4-speed manual
Design = Frank Feeley, H J Mulliner/Tickford
Built = 1953-59

The DB2/4 MkII, however, is not the best of the breed to drive. That honour is reserved for the 1957 revision, the MkIII. Whilst keeping the luxury refinements of the previous models, the MkIII altered the body style, becoming less decorated and more reminiscent of the DB3S sports car. Aston Martin's racing engineers, Harold Beach and Tadek Marek, improved the engine on racing lines. The new engine, the DBA, put out up to 162bph in 'Vantage' tune. The dashboard became more driver-focused too, placing all the instruments behind the steering wheel in a stepped arrangement that continued through to the DB6. Like the Bentley Continental, the MkIII was driven by the literary incarnation of James Bond in *Goldfinger*, sparking an association that continues today.

The DB2/4 began showing its age came when the DBC Competition tune of the engine, producing 214bhp, stretched the ability of the chassis, and it became evident from the larger, Superleggera-constructed Italian machines from the likes of Lancia and Maserati that a new era of grand touring was dawning. Aston Martin's answer was the DB4, which is covered later, but the DB2/4 can be seen as marking the point when Aston Martin truly came of age.

The concept of a hinging rear hatch and folding rear seats concealed in an unbroken fastback profile was adopted by many

Jaguar XK140 & XK150 fhc

In 1948, Jaguar's XK120 sports car turned the motoring world on its head. So soon after the ravages of war, the car that replaced the MG T-Series as the perfect sports car in the eyes of the Americans was a sweeping beauty, the design of which recalled pre-war Art Deco masterpieces and advanced sports-racers alike. The fact that it could be bought for a bargain price compared to all other competitors and offered a class-beating (for the price) 120mph+ performance meant that both the glamorous roadster and the sleek 2-seater coupé sold in the tens of thousands, and the perfectly proportioned style just could not be faulted.

Competition drivers loved them too. The Appleyards won the

SPECIFICATION
CYLINDERS = 6
CAPACITY (LITRES) = 3.4-3.8
POWER = 160-265BHP
TOP SPEED = 124-136MPH
TRANSMISSION = 4-SPEED MANUAL/3-SPEED AUTOMATIC
DESIGN = WILLIAM LYONS, JAGUAR IN-HOUSE
BUILT = 1954-61

RAC rally with the famous 'NUB 120'. The competition variant XK120C (known as the 'C-type') won Le Mans at the hands of Stirling Moss, and was the first of its kind to feature 4-wheel disc brakes, a crucial factor in its victory.

It was, however, still a sports car as opposed to a Grand Tourer, and this was evident in its Spartan cockpit, scant provision for refinement on the roadster, cramped confines of the coupé and a rather 'vintage' driving position reminiscent of the pre-war Jaguar SS100, so much so that, in the modern age, there are a raft of specialists dedicated to making the XK120, that purest example of the breed, more usable.

That is not to say that Jaguar itself did not try, and certainly not without success. Perhaps spurred on by a stretched XK120 four-seat convertible one-off by Abbot coachbuilders, the 1954 replacement for the XK120, the XK140, was geared far more towards spacious continental touring. Reshaped seats made for greater legroom and more comfort. The drophead coupé (as opposed to roadster) featured a much more watertight hood, the boot now featured a fold-down panel into the cockpit, and an automatic transmission option was introduced to take some of the effort out of slotting the lever through the often imprecise Moss gearbox.

The biggest step towards GT motoring came, however, with the altering of the internal bulkheads for greater room, and the fitting of two rear seats in the coupé. Coupled with the natural smoothness of the XK engine and the unsurpassed ride quality on the steel chassis, the XK140 fixed head coupé in particular made for a fine GT car, probably more accomplished than the equivalent Aston Martin.

Although it was moved further from its competition bent, the XK140 was treated to a number of racing-inspired modifications. The B-type featured the disc brakes of the C-type and a racing-tuned cylinder head block to accompany the refinements.

Jaguar's XK140 range built upon the strengths of the rawer, competition-orientated XK120, sporting heavier brightwork, small rear seats, and more luxurious interior appointments. (Courtesy Paul Abadjian)

In the 1950s, as today, often a corporate 'look', inspired by one bestseller in the range, is forced upon the rest of its brethren in an attempt to unify the marque's image. The XK150 of 1957 can be seen as an example of this, with its wider grille, higher waistline and curved, one-piece windscreen chiming with the featured design details of the then-new MkI saloon. Although detrimental to the taut XK140's looks, the bigger bodyshell made for a more comfortable touring experience, even if it now resembled a two-door MkI saloon in coupé form.

The race-winning 3.8-litre MkII saloon of 1959 lent its engine to the XK150, bringing it up-to-date (the previous 3.4-litre

THE PERFECTLY PROPORTIONED STYLE JUST COULD NOT BE FAULTED.

incarnation had been in existence since the war), although fuel economy took a tumble: whereas 22-25 miles per gallon had been the norm in the XK120 and 140, the reality of the XK150 was closer to 18. The XK150S was endowed with straight ports and three carburettors pushing the top speed up to 136mph, making it the fastest road-going variant of the XK-series.

By the 1960s it became clear that the XK150, despite its speed, was not representative of Jaguar's sports-orientated thinking and the more aerodynamic D-type racer-inspired XKE

The XK150 drew its styling from Jaguar's 2.4/3.4 saloon range, with a wider grille, curved windscreen and higher waistline. Many believe these styling revisions spoilt the purity of the early XK form.
(Courtesy David Hodges Collection)

(aka E-type) emerged in 1961, instantly confining the XK150 to the history books, although they were, and still are, perfect British Grand Tourers.

The roomier 150 reflected the car's more comfortable touring nature.
(Courtesy David Hodges Collection)

21

Facel Vega FVS/HK500

Jean Daninos' first car design was an exquisitely re-bodied Bentley MkVI, built with staggering attention to detail, from the exhausts concealed in the back bumper to the painted wood-effect dashboard (a weight-saving measure that was actually more expensive to finish than using walnut veneer). Many features of that one-off Bentley, such as the imposing, upright grille, stacked headlights and subtle fins topped with fluted tail-lights, would make it onto the later Facel Vega cars.

Facel (Forges et Atiliers de Construction d'Eure et Loire), a manufacturing plant in the Loire valley, turned its attention to cars at the behest of controlling industrialist Daninos after successfully providing the bodies for Ford of France's rare Cometé. Unlike many 'start-up' car companies, Daninos' intention was only ever to make the finest GT cars in the world. Traditional, expensive bodywork and chassis manufacturing techniques, Facel's trademark artwork interiors and exquisite trimming made it into the FVS (Facel Vega Sportif), although Daninos found himself without a thoroughbred engine of his own to fit to the car. No European GT company would lend him the means to usurp their dominance of the genre, and few readily accessible volume-produced French, British, German or Italian blocks possessed the refinement necessary to take on the likes of Bentley.

The answer was Chrysler. American automotive isolationism had meant that American engines, along with the cars they were attached to, had developed to suit American roads and tastes. Vast distances needed to be traversed, home-produced fuel was cheap, roads were straight and smooth, and, as a result, American engines, in particular the V8s, were smooth, torque-laden, relaxing to control and very, very powerful.

Taken out of the wallowing, softly sprung American chassis and installed in the Vega, the Chrysler V8 was a revelation. It provided the power of a Bentley Continental, with comparable cruising ability, but with reliability and serviceability on its side. If a Bentley failed to proceed, the precision-built engine was so expensive and rare that few mechanics would be able to maintain it. The Chrysler V8, on the other hand was commonplace on the other side of the Atlantic, as ubiquitous as Jaguar's XK, probably more so, making for more relaxed ownership and a certain indomitable feeling brought with the realisation that, even if the Vega did break down, someone would most likely know how to fix it.

SPECIFICATION
Cylinders = V8
Capacity (litres) = 4.5-6.3
Power = 355-390bhp
Top speed = 125-130mph
Transmission = 4-speed manual/3-speed automatic
Design = Jean Daninos, Facel
Built = 1954-61
Innovation: first GT to use a stock American V8

The styling of French industrialist Jean Daninos' Facel-Vega was inspired by both British and American themes, reflecting its intended market, and the origins of its engine. (Courtesy David Hodges Collection)

On the road, the Facel Vega was fast, stable and refined, proving that thoroughbred origins were not necessarily a prerequisite for rivalling Bentley. (Courtesy David Hodges Collection)

During the 1950s, Facel experimented with a whole raft of V8s on its FVS, starting with a relatively small (by American standards) 4.5-litre, then graduating through 4.8s, 5.4s and 5.8s, before settling on the definitive Chrysler 6.3-litre big-block in the Vega HK500 of 1959. This engine was to be the watershed, as it, and similar-sized engines from different American manufacturers would go on to find themselves installed on so many European GT cars throughout the 1960s; Iso, Jensen, Montiverdi, Gordon-Keeble and DeTomaso would all go on to build their reputations around cheap American power wrapped in European sophistication. The trend traversed the boundaries of the GT car too, the ultimate expression of Euro-American hybrid supercars being the AC Cobra and DeTomaso Pantera. All these cars make

for a more cost-effective and trouble-free route to GT motoring, and these big, simple units are more easily adapted to run on cleaner, cheaper liquid petroleum gas (LPG) fuels than race-tuned supercar power plants, so their usability factor continues. Their 'mongrel' image also helps keep the prices down: a Facel Vega is worth less than half of a Bentley Continental today.

The Facel Vega HK500 bowed out in 1961, giving way to the far more modern-looking Facel II, which also made for a better competitor to the many hybrid GTs it had spawned: it ditched the HK500s drum brakes for discs for a start, and the Detroit-inspired wraparound reverse-angle windscreen also went. In short, although Facel had set the ball rolling, it had to run more quickly to avoid complacency, a factor that killed it in the end.

Jensen 541

The Jensen 541 has many automotive 'firsts' to its name – the first fibreglass-bodied four-seater, the fastest four-seater of the 1950s, the most aerodynamic car in 1954 – but these were simply by-products of the designers' intention to create a consummate GT car built on many British automotive mainstays of the 1950s 'specials' era, but improved in terms of power, volume production and quality.

Jensen had been, pre-war, a builder of touring saloons to rival Lagonda, its flagship S-Type being elegant and powerful, yet never as popular as its compatriot rivals. This new GT car had to be something completely different, or Jensen would not survive. It had, however, a limited budget, so could not coach-build the bodies and craft the engines as per arch rivals Aston Martin and Bristol. Jensen's thinking turned to the booming specials movement for inspiration.

The typical British 'special' of the 1950s could be typified by the early kit-built offerings of TVR, Marcos and Lotus (later to graduate to the realm of the supercar and the GT themselves). The basis would often be a family car, usually a 1.2-litre Ford Popular. The car would be stripped of its bodywork and a new, sporting bodyshell would endow the usually asthmatic Ford side-valve unit with better performance brought on by its lighter weight and aerodynamic design. This laid the foundations for the British sports car, and the most renowned names from this era used superior chassis technology to produce race winners. Lotus built its reputation for the world's best-handling cars from its roots as a builder of racing chassis.

Jensen had to upsize the concept. Taking the Rolls-Royce-designed 4-litre straight six from an Austin Sheerline and hooking it up through a high-geared Rolls-Royce gearbox the recipe was perfect for touring. Using many stock Austin parts from higher up the range, such as the drum brakes and suspension components from an A70, kept the price down both for Jensen and the buyers.

The bodywork, however, explored new territory aerodynamically. Eric Neale incorporated blisters over the wheelarches in an aerofoil shape to prevent the trailing edge of the arch from spoiling the airflow. All lamps were smoothed-off and faired-in and, most strikingly, a large cover over the radiator regulated the amount of air required, folding backwards at higher speeds, yet maintaining airflow over the nose. All these refinements led to a 0.39 drag coefficient, still commendable today, complementing a high speed coupled with manageable fuel economy thanks to the (light) 50:50 weight distribution and efficiently smooth transmission. The tuned Austin DS7 541R variant of 1957 was the fastest four-seater car available for a while, a title that embarrassed the likes of Aston Martin and Jaguar, with their race-proven and traditionally-engineered, yet frequently less accommodating rival products.

SPECIFICATION
CYLINDERS = 6
CAPACITY (LITRES) = 4.0
POWER = 150BHP
TOP SPEED = 123-125MPH
TRANSMISSION = 4-SPEED AUTOMATIC OVERDRIVE
DESIGN = ERIC NEALE, JENSEN IN-HOUSE
BUILT = 1954-63

Stagnation eventually got the better of Jensen with the 1961-63 541S. These cars were designed to be less fussy and more 'mainstream', losing many of the endearing qualities of the 541 and 541R, and the 4-litre Austin engine was getting old. Jensen's way out of this particular mire was to follow Facel practise and redesign around a cheap, powerful American V8 with the CV8. This re-start policy revitalised Jensen in 1962, only to sink it in the oil crisis and recession of 1974.

Today, the Jensen 541 series, and the 541R in particular, makes for the most usable Jensen Grand Tourer until the GT of 1973, with its manageable economy, reasonable pricing, basic engine, and rust-free bodyshell. Renowned classic car writer Martin Buckley paid it the ultimate compliment in 2003 when he wrote: "it's hard to think of anything that does so much so well for so little."

BMW 503

Mentioning BMW in the context of the 1950s brings up the most schizophrenic of images. On one hand is the tiny Isetta 'bubble car', licence-built in an attempt to revive the flagging fortunes of BMW and contend with growing fears of an energy crisis, and on the other is the Hollywood glamour of the 507 roadster as owned by such stars as Elvis Presley and Ursula Andress, built in tiny numbers at huge prices, reflected today in their list price of over £100,000.

But there is, as in any situation with BMW, some overshadowed middle ground, and it is here that we find our 1950s Grand Tourer, the 503. Though it may lack the gravitas of the styling of the 507, or the trend-setting, Jaguar-influencing styling of its 'parent' saloon, the 1952-63 5-series 'baroque angel', the clean, well-proportioned coupé shape and potent power of the BMW V8 make it impossible to overlook in a celebration of the Grand Tourer.

Despite costing much less, due to its production-line origins, the 503 shared most of its basic components with the 507. Launched a year later than the roadster in an effort to bridge the gap between sports car and saloon with a GT, the 507 was strongly influenced by Lancia and Alfa Romeo. It had high, protruding single headlamps at either side, a bold grille and a crisp, clean notchback shape, penned by the 507's designer, Albrecht Goertz, to forge a link between the likes of the 507 and the other BMW designs of the Italian Giovanni Michelotti (who, alongside some Ferrari racing cars, busied himself designing the rest of BMW's small car range as well as the more successful British Triumph cars, which BMW sought to beat).

THE CLEAN, WELL-PROPORTIONED COUPÉ SHAPE AND POTENT POWER OF THE BMW V8 MAKE IT IMPOSSIBLE TO OVERLOOK IN A CELEBRATION OF THE

the driving experience was not overtly sporting in the way the comparable Mercedes-Benz 300SL was, but its saloon-like responses coupled with the greater rigidity of the coupé body and a plusher, more accommodating cabin made for a much better Grand Tourer. You could quite happily exploit the handling of a 503 on a twisty Alpine road much more readily than you could in a 507 or a Mercedes-Benz SL, laying down BMWs precedent for handling sophistication with subtlety.

SPECIFICATION
CYLINDERS = V8
CAPACITY (LITRES) = 3.2
POWER = 150BHP
TOP SPEED = 115MPH
TRANSMISSION = 4-SPEED MANUAL
DESIGN = COUNT ALBRECHT GOERTZ
BUILT = 1956-59

Perhaps the 503's greatest legacy was the bloodline of BMW coupés it spawned. With BMWs new influx of wealth throughout the 1960s, greater development of the concepts could be afforded, ensuring a dynasty of distinctive Grand Tourers through the CS-Series (the first of which, the ultra-rare 3200CS, featured stop-gap styling by Bertone and borrowed heavily from the 503 mechanically), 6-Series and 8-Series to today's revitalised 6-Series, with fuss-free, glassy styling remaining a constant throughout.

However, in the terms of the 1950s – and the classic market today – the 507 hogged too much of the limelight, even though the 503 was probably the better car, with improved handling, accommodation and overall ability over the roadster, despite continued development on the 507 pushing it to 160bhp and

With its 3.2-litre V8 and strong, safe roadholding tendencies, the 503 was the glamorous 507 roadster's bigger, more practical sister. It launched a dynasty of BMW GT cars that continues in today's Bangle-styled 6-series. (Courtesy David Hodges Collection)

Alvis TD21

In a rapidly modernising world of exotic Aston Martins and futuristic Jensens dominating the grand touring headlines, the Alvis TD21 looked rather an anachronism. From its radiator grille that harked back to more rakish times, and its casual sops to traditionalism, such as the barely noticeable kick-up over the rear arches reminiscent of the flowing wings of pre-war tourers, there was nothing remotely fashionable about the TD21.

Yet it was this traditionalism that perhaps ensured its success. In the 1950s, the grand touring market was not all about exoticism and the white heat of technology, but solid values and middle-class respectability – values thoroughly embraced by Alvis. As a company previously renowned for its touring roadsters beloved of racing drivers (Malcolm Campbell owned a Speed 25) and their unfailing reliability (an early promise to customers was that the company would pay them £1 for every day the car was being repaired), Alvis customers had massive expectations of a new Grand Tourer to take on the best that the likes of Bristol had to offer.

Alvis' position was unique in the British car market. Its dedication to quality and reliability put it just below Rolls-Royce

and Bentley in the opulence stakes, yet the rather staid technology, unsporting (for the modern age) construction and unexciting road manners placed the cars just above Rover in terms of enjoyment for the sporting driver. All in all, the TD21 was a rather middle-aged prospect. Yet grand touring is not about outright speed and lightning handling, and the TD21's solid traction and torque-biased power delivery allowed an unruffled cruise to one's destination. Manual transmission options maintained a sense of driver focus in the design, but this car was primarily about travelling in the most agreeable fashion possible.

Adapting a design from Swiss design house Graber, Alvis' traditional coachbuilding methods dictated a commissioned firm manufacture the bodies. The TC108G, as the first prototypes were named (built on a TC chassis, 108mph, Graber design), emerged from Loughborough's Willowbrooks coachworks in 1956, but did not meet the letter of Alvis' law in terms of the firm's commitment to the utmost quality, and the contract fell to Park Ward of London, concurrently providing bodies for the Bentley Continental (most likely an aspirational car in the eyes of an Alvis owner). Park Ward continued to build the TD21's successors up until the demise of Alvis' car-building operations in 1967, probably making it the last volume manufacturer to approach car building in this way.

The TD21 made a few attempts to keep up with the modern crowd. With one eye on the Aston Martin DB2/4 and Jaguar XK150, Alvis equipped the 1962 SII version with four-wheel disc brakes and fitted a ZF gearbox with an extra cog to stretch the TD21's legs a little more. Although rather sluggish in the face of XK-powered Jaguars and the new wave of V8-equipped GTs, the new gearbox allowed the TD21 to cruise higher up in its 110mph range, though times had changed by 1963, and the need for Alvis to change with them was becoming all too evident.

In terms of today's grand touring, the Alvis TD21 is rather a stately machine in comparison to its contemporaries, and must be treated with the required respect, although the toughness (Alvis' main concern was military vehicles) and simplicity of its construction makes it a more serviceable prospect for a competent mechanic than its more adventurous rivals.

SPECIFICATION
CYLINDERS = 6
CAPACITY (LITRES) = 3.0
POWER = 115BHP
TOP SPEED = 102MPH
TRANSMISSION = 4/5-SPEED MANUAL/3-SPEED AUTOMATIC
DESIGN = GRABER, PARK WARD
BUILT = 1956-63

Opposite: Stately looks and an imposing stance are somewhat at odds with the coachbuilt Alvis TD21's handling and performance.
(Courtesy David Hodges Collection)

Period advertising highlighted the practicalities of this four-seat coupé and convertible. Note the rear wings still bearing the then-anachronistic curve behind the doors.
(Courtesy David Hodges Collection)

Alfa Romeo Giulietta SS & Giulia SS

Alfa Romeo's SS could comfortably be described as Italy's Jensen 541. The concepts of going back to a country's sports car roots, refining them, adding the new 1950s science of aerodynamics and relying on stock parts to produce an accidental record-breaking GT – in Alfa's case, the fastest 1.3-litre car for a time – and simultaneously generating part of a flagship model range to turn around the fortunes of an ailing company (nowadays termed a 'halo effect') through volume sales runs true through both Alfa Romeo and Jensen at this time.

Before the Giulietta series of cars, Alfa Romeo was known for

its Enzo Ferrari-fettled racing cars, pre-war Art Deco statements such as the 8C 2900B, and indulgent super-luxury saloons such as the Freccia d'Oro and Villa d'Este (featured in *The Godfather*) – now blue-chip classics for the very rich and owned by the likes of rock star Eric Clapton. In the 1950s, however, Alfa Romeo could not continue with such a highfalutin design brief, and its 'Alfa Romeo for the people' – the Giulietta range, initially comprising a Berlina (Saloon) and Sprint Berlinetta sports coupé – went on to sell enthusiastically in Italy and in large numbers throughout Europe. Many, especially the Giulietta Sprint, were professionally raced.

It was the success of the Sprint Veloce sports coupé in racing, and the creation of a lightweight version by Zagato – the SZ – that inspired aerodynamicist and Bertone stylist Franco Scaglione to experiment with ideas on the Giulietta platform. The Bertone BAT (Berlinetta Aerodynamica Technica, literally 'aerodynamic technology coupé') series and Alfa's own Giulietta Spider-based Disco Volante factory racer involved the creation of extremely streamlined shapes using low winglines, blistered wheelarches and air manipulation through embryonic spoilers. Released between 1953 and 1955, the BAT series – 5, 7 and 9 – also used unusual 'show car' cues mixed with racing car thinking. The

SPECIFICATION
CYLINDERS = 4
CAPACITY (LITRES) = 1.3-1.6
POWER = 80-90BHP
TOP SPEED = 122-125MPH
TRANSMISSION = 5-SPEED MANUAL
DESIGN = FRANCO SCAGLIONE, BERTONE
BUILT = 1957-66

The sleek lines of the beautiful SS Giulietta and Giulia were inspired by Bertone's BAT (Berlinetta Aerodynamica Technica) series of concept cars. (Courtesy David Hodges Collection)

Light weight, superb aerodynamics, and excellent handling made the SS a good competition choice. (Courtesy David Hodges Collection)

The low, crisp outline of the SS would inspire a new generation of small-engined GT cars from the likes of Lotus. (Courtesy David Hodges Collection)

The Kamm-tail at the rear of the SS was an influential design feature that reduced turbulence, inspired a new sports car convention, and was the ancestor of the ubiquitous rear spoiler. (Courtesy Stuart Pugh)

forged his reputation with racing chassis adapted for Fords and Austins. The SS used this heritage, utilising the optional five-speed gearbox and high-revving twin-cam design of the Giulietta 101-series engine. Thanks once again to the bodywork, it could hit 60mph in 10.5 seconds. Trimmed stylishly and comfortably by Enrico Nardi, the SS was a competent Grand Tourer, coming into its own on twisting Alpine passes on trans-European jaunts whilst probably being the most fuel efficient of the class in this period.

The march of time dictated its modification. The Giulietta series was ousted by the 1962 Giulia series, which lent its 1.6-litre engine to the 1963 incarnation of the SS. This new unit gave more torque and power, but its weight blunted the impact of the lighter SS. Despite now hitting 60mph in 10 seconds flat, the top speed was closer to 120mph. However, given the popularity of the Spider convertible, the lower price of the Sprint coupé and the greater appeal to racing drivers of Zagato's SZ, the Giulia SS was nowhere near as popular as its forebear. Production tailed off in 1965, and only one Giulia SS was completed in 1966, by which time Bertone's new Giulia GT had replaced the SS as the Italian motorist's GT of choice, but that is another story.

Today, the unsullied design-house lines of the SS, coupled with an engine that is, even by modern standards, cheap to maintain and run, make it an extremely enticing prospect for a 1950s GT revivalist, although its comparative rarity and those sublime looks will always ensure high prices.

BAT 7, with styling similar to the streamlined, high-tech Lotus MkIX, featured headlights that popped sideways out of the inner front wings.

BAT 9, however, was a much more cohesive design with production firmly in its sights. In 1957, the Giulietta Sprint Speciale prototype was revealed at the Turin show scheduled for immediate production as the SS, intended to turn the Giulietta series into a truly competent Grand Tourer. From just 1.3 litres, the Giulietta SS managed 125mph, thanks to a 0.29 drag coefficient. It reached volume production in 1959.

Like the Jensen 541, Alfa Romeo went to Italy's car roots to build the ideal GT. Whilst British sports cars were largely about fibreglass bodies and thorough race-proven chassis engineering, Italy had a noble tradition of engineering and tuning race engines for private customers: Enzo Ferrari built his reputation upon racing Alfa Romeo engines in the same way that Lotus' Colin Chapman

Zagato's take on the SS, the SZ, was initially controversial but took the aerodynamics to an even more advanced level, and inspired Alfa's own in-house Duetto Spider. (Courtesy Stuart Pugh)

Aston Martin DB4

To many connoisseurs, the Aston Martin DB4 is and will always be the ultimate GT car. Not only did it set a precedent for Aston Martin's design and performance that still exists today, it set trends throughout Europe with its sharp, well-proportioned styling by Touring of Milano, provided the quintessential GT car for fans of the continent-crossing breed, introduced a previously unseen combination of opulence and road handling (previous GTs had frequently been a trade-off between upright, ponderous luxury or functionality coupled with a more involving drive), and found victories among the sports car races of Europe.

The DB4 was also adaptable. Later, racing-specification engines could be coupled with a variety of interpretations on the bodywork to produce a car that was as much at home on the racetrack as on the motorway. More powerful Vantage and GT versions sought to intensify the GT experience, bringing even more urgency and sharpness to the package – something the original wasn't exactly short of. The DB4's derivatives include Le Mans challengers, experimental racers and even a Formula 1 car. It is hard to stress, in this day and age of screaming 200mph supercars how much of a landmark this car really was.

The DB4 story begins with a prototype replacement for the DB2/4 MkIII. Styled by Frank Feeley, its styling seemed dated alongside Touring Milano's proposal. The smooth yet crisp design provided unquestionable modernity to the Aston Martin concept, whilst details worked on by Federico Formenti enhanced cues from previous Astons: the new vent in the wing echoed the chrome strake and stylised door handles of the DB2 series. The subtle hump in the boot to maintain the fastback line recalled the 2/4, and the full-width grille still carried that central 'step' that links all Aston Martins.

Released in 1958 to a rapturous public and press, the DB4 was the ultimate in grand touring. Despite an early reputation for overheating in traffic, it was largely reliable. The new, stiffer

SPECIFICATION
CYLINDERS = 6
CAPACITY (LITRES) = 3.7-4.2
POWER = 240-350BHP
TOP SPEED = 140-155MPH
TRANSMISSION = 4-SPEED MANUAL
DESIGN = SNR BIANCHI & FEDERICO FORMENTI, TOURING, & ERCOLE SPADA, ZAGATO
BUILT = 1958-63 (SOME GT ZAGATOS COMPLETED 1989)

The elegant, Italianate DB4 was the first of the Touring-designed Aston Martins. (Courtesy David Hodges Collection)

intermediary between standard and racing specification. The rarest of DB4 Vantages were fitted with GT engines, this 'Vantage GT' being the ultimate in both performance and luxury, and probably the best of the DB4s to drive and own.

The DB4 story does not end there. In response to the refinement of Ferrari cars in the early 1960s, both on the track and on the road, Aston Martin boss David Brown commissioned an even more exotic DB4GT, bodied by Zagato. Designed to take on the Ferrari 250 SWB whilst providing more refinement, the DB4GT Zagato emerged in 1960. Although it under-performed on track and its price when new made it prohibitive to sell, its rarity and sheer beauty ensures its current

Superleggera build (a technique involving rolled aluminium panels over a box-section chassis carrying thin steel tubes to shape the body) meant much-improved high-speed handling over that of the DB2/4, and greater strength within the shell itself: it could quite clearly cope with more power. Although Aston Martin offered a Vantage version in a mildly higher state of tune, the DB4GT – a lightweight model inspired by R S Williams' race-prepared DB4s, was seen as the way forward. Featuring faired-in lights for aerodynamics and no bumpers or rear seats (alongside other small details) for lighter weight, the GT, with its twin-sparkplug engine, touring-specification fuel tank filling the boot and lowered suspension became the ultimate option for those intending to both race and tour. Evolution of the Vantage models was dictated by the DB4GT: cowled headlights and slightly lower, firmer suspension made the DB4 Vantage a faster

price is well into the millions. The car became so sought after, in fact, that some 'Sanction 2' Zagatos were completed on DB4GT chassis in 1989, at the height of the investment-car boom. These are the fastest DB4s, with twin-plug, 4.2-litre engines producing 350bhp. Many other 'replicas' have been constructed, but none have been quite so perfect as the Sanction 2.

The DB4 stands alone as a benchmark GT car, although its legacy stretches further. The Vantage engine was slotted straight into the DBR4 Formula 1 car with little modification. The car itself went on to form the basis of the DP212 experimental racer, and its styling proportions and abilities were carried on to every Aston Martin since. Its greatest recognition factor, however, is marred by misrepresentation: it was in fact a DB4 Series 5 Vantage, and not a DB5, that was driven by Sean Connery in *Goldfinger*.

Maserati 3500GT/GTI

Maserati could easily be said to be Italy's Aston Martin. With an eye more on luxury, subtlety and refinement than the raw V12 thrust of compatriot Ferrari, the similarity of designs – both mechanically and aesthetically – has made for easy comparisons between the Italian and British firms for many years. The 3500GT can be seen to be where it all started: the Maserati 3500GT is Italy's Aston Martin DB4.

Like Aston Martin and Ferrari, Maserati began by making highly successful racing machines, with sporting road cars a thrilling, if Spartan prospect. The Maserati A6GS sports car had been bodied by all manner of Italian coachbuilders and had raced in club events with some degree of success. In bigger leagues, Maserati's iconic 250F took the Formula 1 world championship title at the hands of Juan-Manuel Fangio in 1957, and the 450S sports-racer, with its savage 4.5-litre V8, was a formidable challenger to the world sports car championship. Odd to think, then, that in 1957 Maserati went into receivership through lack of funds. A more commercial offering was required to keep the Trident marque alive.

MUCH SMOOTHER THAN A FERRARI, SUMPTUOUSLY TRIMMED BY NARDI AND JAEGER, AND PROVIDING SOLID TRACTION THROUGH ITALY'S COUNTRY ROUTES, IT BECAME A SAVIOUR IN THE EYES OF MASERATI.

Giulio Alfieri designed the 3500GT coupé hurriedly inside and out, completing a prototype from scratch in 1957. It is no surprise that Touring's design, which he overlooked, bore more than a passing resemblance to the Aston Martin DB4, quite fittingly as it turned out. The 3.5-litre twin-cam straight six was derived from racing practise and detuned, though it could be related directly to that found in Fangio's racing car. The 3500GT met with instant success, buoying Maserati out of receivership and into profit. Giovanni Michelotti's 1959 convertible proposal

met with approval, boosting sales in America to add to its natural market of grand touring in Europe.

As a GT, the 3500GT was as capable as an early Aston Martin DB4. Much smoother than a Ferrari, sumptuously trimmed by Nardi and Jaeger, and providing solid traction through Italy's country routes, it became a saviour in the eyes of Maserati, which could not have predicted its popularity. Volume sales were welcomed with open arms.

SPECIFICATION
CYLINDERS = 6
CAPACITY (LITRES) = 3.5
POWER = 220-235BHP
TOP SPEED = 127-129MPH
TRANSMISSION = 4-SPEED MANUAL
DESIGN = GIULIO ALFIERI & GIOVANNI MICHELOTTI, TOURING
BUILT = 1958-63

Unlike the DB4, however, its development was rather limited. At 127mph, its top speed did not make headlines like the DB4's. Although some were privately prepared for racing, it was not developed by the factory for that purpose (all available money went into production rather than development), and the 3500GT, worthy though it was, did not enjoy the accolade of a DB4GT equivalent.

Salvation arrived in the form of the new technology of fuel injection. The 3500GTI (the first time this term was used, despite Volkswagen's insistence) emerged in 1962, carrying a few Michelotti-penned detail improvements too. Fuel injection made for an even smoother touring experience, but as an early technology, the indirect-injection system was not as reliable as Maserati had hoped, although it did raise the top speed to closer to 130mph. Fast, perfect for GT motoring, but not enough to catch a speeding Aston Martin.

In the end, a financially revitalised Maserati decided to replace the 3500GT rather than updating it: the Sebring being more of a consummate GT car and the race-engined 5-litre

The Maserati 3500GT, in Michelotti-designed, Vignale-built Spider guise. (Courtesy David Hodges Collection)

5000GT being a two-seater supercar. Fast and slightly unruly, the 5000GT pointed the way to such classic Maserati supercars as the Ghibli and the Khamsin, but by this stage the Maserati range was very much divided into Grand Tourers and racers, a separation that has continued, with a few blips, to this day.

Today, the 3500GT makes for an intriguing and exotic alternative to a more expensive Aston Martin DB4, and its slightly more pedestrian nature, less well-known image and relatively short life-span make for prices reflecting greater value for money than the Aston, too.

AC Greyhound

Britain's oldest car manufacturer AC has always been best known for its sports cars: the Ace, Aceca and Cobra. Its other sidelines – saloons, invalid carriages and GT cars – are more often than not forgotten, perhaps by AC itself (which still makes the Cobra), in favour of an image dominated by traditional British roadsters and monumental American V8 hybrid muscle cars.

But this image of AC cannot be complete without the Grand Tourers. In the 1950s and 1960s, AC attracted the jet set as well as the racing drivers, and the first foray into refinement and sophistication was the Greyhound of 1959. In construction, the Greyhound was classic AC, sharing its drivetrain with the Ace and Aceca sports cars, but unlike its raw natured brethren, it was trimmed in the finest leather and wood, enjoyed a two-plus-two seating arrangement and a higher level of sound deadening. The four-speed overdrive transmission, optional on the sports cars, was standard on the Greyhound in the name of cruising ability, and the car retained the sharp handling manners of the Ace that endeared it to both the public and the likes of tuners Ken Rudd and Carroll Shelby.

Another feature that set the Greyhound apart was its use of a mixture of aluminium and fibreglass for the bodywork, a weight-saving factor that allowed the Bristol engine to stretch its legs, although the additional weight of the trimming and sheer size over the comparable Bristol-powered Aceca showed in an overall top speed which was a full 10mph slower. Overall speed, as in all GTs, was not the point – refinement was, and the Greyhound had it in spades.

The ride, like all ACs, was pliant, although the saloon-like nature of the Greyhound made for a smoother experience than the Ace

series. Perhaps it was this feeling of detachment that failed to endear the Greyhound to the public. That and the price – it cost nearly £1000 more than the Aceca, a difference that a casual glance at the two cars in the dealers might not have justified.

In the end, the fate of the AC Greyhound was all a question of image. The average AC customer paid for sporting thrills, not grand touring refinement. The success of the Ace in competition, and the genus of the Cobra, a true legend of the road and track by anybody's standards, seemed to undermine AC's image as a builder of grand touring cars to rival Aston Martin. Although

SPECIFICATION
CYLINDERS = 6
CAPACITY (LITRES) = 2.0
POWER = 125BHP
TOP SPEED = 107MPH
TRANSMISSION = 4-SPEED MANUAL OVERDRIVE
DESIGN = JOHN TOJEIRO, AC IN-HOUSE
BUILT = 1959-63

Mechanically, the Greyhound borrowed much from the Ace/Aceca roadster/coupé range. (Courtesy Martin Brewer)

The AC Greyhound was innovative in its use of fibreglass, but customers preferred the more sporting, less practical AC models.
(Courtesy David Hodges Collection)

the later Cobra-based 428 enjoyed greater success, AC was still being buoyed up by the Cobra. Later AC attempts to launch Grand Tourers (particularly the new Ace in 1988) failed due to

OVERALL SPEED, AS IN ALL GTS, WAS NOT THE POINT — REFINEMENT WAS, AND THE GREYHOUND HAD IT IN SPADES.

lack of demand compared to the Cobra, so perhaps it just is not within the lore of this company.

Today, the AC Greyhound enjoys a rather happier fate. It is seen, due to its looks and heritage, as a lower-priced alternative to the Aston Martin DB2/4, and its GT refinements are seen as a positive contribution to a car that is able to manage a reasonable continental tour, especially with a usable and reliable 2-litre Bristol engine and rust-free bodywork. In terms of AC, however, it is still unfairly remembered, perhaps, as the car that wasn't the Cobra.

Lancia Flaminia Coupé/GT

Quite possibly the very height of good taste, Lancia's Flaminia was one of the first GTs to bring Gran Turismo motoring out of the rarified atmosphere it had found itself in previously and into a far more accessible market. That said, it was still expensive enough to put it out of the reach of the majority. In modern terms, it was to the late 1950s and early 1960s what a BMW 6-Series is to the 2000s – highly exclusive, yet not rare enough to draw a crowd. It was the first taste for many of GT ownership.

Based around a saloon, as so many volume-built GTs are (in this case the 1957 Flaminia), in order to provide tried and tested components to avoid excessive costs, this car was known under a vast variety of guises depending on engine and bodywork. A highly advanced Lancia V6 was standard all round, providing an even mixture of smoothness and high revs (once Lancia became part of the FIAT group in 1969, the refinement of its V6 engines bore fruit across the range, so acclaimed was its expertise in this field).

Producing 119bhp with a single carburettor in its first incarnation, the Flaminia Coupé enjoyed a raft of engine options as befitted a commercial, volume-produced GT. Borrowing heavily from the saloon (though with a shorter, stiffer floorplan geared towards grand touring), faster early variants of the Flaminia Coupé had American-inspired Solex three-barrel carburettors producing 126bhp, although the weight of the car did little to aid the 2.5-litre V6 in propelling this heavy car to 115mph.

Heavy and slow compared to more expensive exotica it may have been, but it led in other areas. The styling, derived from the Lancia Florida series of show cars, was prophetic in its sharpness, with only details such as the large single headlights and receding fins eventually dating its styling to the 1950s. V6 engines would eventually replace straight sixes as the mid-sized engine of choice among manufacturers, and the precise way it handled – taut and unassisted yet without being harsh or overly sporting – was admired by many as a benchmark in chassis engineering.

It was the lack of urge that was beginning to worry Lancia, though, and in 1963 the car received a re-working as the Flaminia GT. A shorter wheelbase, a 2.8-litre upgrade of the V6 raising power to 136bhp, plus twin headlights at each side for safer night driving made the Flaminia GT a contender again, although the lack of torque from such a rev-biased engine let it down as a cruiser. Its image, however, could never be faulted.

SPECIFICATION
CYLINDERS = V6
CAPACITY (LITRES) = 2.5-2.8
POWER = 119-128BHP
TOP SPEED = 112-130MPH
TRANSMISSION = 4-SPEED MANUAL
DESIGN = BATTISTA PININFARINA, PININFARINA/ERCOLE SPADA, ZAGATO
BUILT = 1959-67

The long-wheelbase Spider version of the Flaminia Coupé offered a good balance of speed, style and practicality. (Courtesy David Hodges Collection)

Lancia was not the only one to try and eke a little more touring capability from the Flaminia. Ercole Spada of Zagato (who also has the Aston Martin DB4GT Zagato to his illustrious credit) designed a lightweight alloy body, reminiscent in some ways of his re-bodied Mini and Hillman Imp-based Zimp, what with its razor-sharp lines and semi-faired headlights and grille. The fastback recalled the DB4GT-Z, and aided by the low 'double bubble' roofline and 2.8-litre V6 in its highest state of tune, the Lancia Flaminia GT Sport Zagato hit a maximum of 130mph, putting it in Maserati 3500GT territory.

Under the pressure of time the Flaminia line bowed out to the Flavia range of 1967, but it was not forgotten. In fact, many stayed in the showrooms until the early 1970s – a result of both high prices and an unshakably dignified image that the Flaminia had over the Flavia.

Today, the Flaminia Coupé and GT make excellent value alternatives to more expensive Maseratis and the like. Their styling and Touring ability recall much more exotic rivals, yet their volume production and saloon basis keep current prices below £10,000. The Sport Zagato is a different story – it always has been – and attracts cognoscenti much more readily: it truly is an exotic rival to Maserati.

Top: With a shorter wheelbase and a taut, rigid roofline, the Flaminia GT offered improved handling for keen drivers. (Courtesy David Hodges Collection)

As was the practice with many Italian sports cars, Zagato stepped in with some superior aerodynamics for the SSZ. (Courtesy David Hodges Collection)

Ferrari 250GTE, GTB Lusso and 330 America

Ferrari's 250 series reads like a motor racing hall of fame: the 250GT Tour De France of the 1950s, winner of many races in private hands; the 250 Testa Rossa, Short-wheelbase, GTO and LM sports-racers all worth well over a million pounds and used to devastating effect on the racing tracks of the world; and the built-to-order supercars that were to build Ferrari's reputation, especially in America – the 250GT California and the PF Coupé and Cabriolet. All perfect investments and glorious fun, if you have the cash.

Big V12s aside, these early 250s might have delivered racing levels of handling, but they were hardly comfortable to travel in. The bare cockpit of a 250SWB, with its boot space filled by a racing fuel tank and a total lack of sound deadening resulted in a constant shriek and thrash from the engine bay, which might have made for the perfect track star, but not the perfect continent-crosser.

Like Maserati, Ferrari realised the need for greater volume sales in order to survive. Building crude racers for teams and showy supercars for the denizens of Hollywood may have given Ferrari credibility in the headlines of the motoring press, but not in its bank accounts. The need to add a usable grand touring car to the model range was evident, and thus the 250GTE was born.

Refining the 250 series led to many innovations within Ferrari, which continue in the 250GTE's reverential descendant, today's 612 Scaglietti. The use of softened telescopic dampers all round made for a sophisticated – and smoother – suspension system for the 250. Unlike the previous Ferrari practise of fitting an engine straight from competition specification into a road car, Giocchino Columbo's venerable V12 was fitted with triple Weber carburettors with external plugs to achieve greater smoothness.

SPECIFICATION
CYLINDERS = V12
CAPACITY (LITRES) = 3.0-4.0
POWER = 235-300BHP
TOP SPEED = 136-152MPH
TRANSMISSION = 4-SPEED MANUAL OVERDRIVE
DESIGN = SERGIO PININFARINA, PININFARINA
BUILT = 1960-63
INNOVATION = CREATED THE FIRST FERRARI GRAND TOURER BY REFINING A RACER

With a 250 California Spider to the right, a line of 250GTEs await customer delivery at Ferrari's Maranello factory. (Courtesy David Hodges Collection)

Transmission-wise, the 250GTE had a special overdrive system installed on its 4-speed gearbox. Automatically actuated, the electric ratio aimed to cut the V12's fuel consumption during prolonged touring use, reducing revs by twenty-two per cent. Although the system was not as reliable as Ferrari had hoped, it was a good consideration for such a thirsty engine considering its grand touring intentions.

Refinement was certainly not confined to the mechanics: the 250GTE was the first Ferrari to be equipped with a proper air heater and cold-air circulation system. Trimmed in the finest leather, the cockpit's finer details, such as the body-coloured metal flash across the dashboard, were picked up by FIAT in the Coupé of 1993. The bodywork was designed with the aid of a wind tunnel to cut down on wind noise for long-distance touring, the tapering tail housing a large boot and two reasonable-sized rear seats.

The 250GTE was the most numerous of the Ferrari 250 series (1000 built), although it has gained infamy in later years: many 250GTEs have been sacrificed for their components, both to keep more valuable 250s running, and to make replicas of such cars as the 250SWB, with which it shares many characteristics.

Unfortunately, these replicas are likely to be worth more than the GTE today.

There is more though – keen to find a niche between the track-focused 250SWB and GTO, and the more lavishly equipped and civilised GTE, Ferrari teamed up with Pininfarina once more for the 250GT Berlinetta Lusso. Resembling a truncated GTE, more lithe and with a squatter stance, plus enticing features like a Kamm-tail and little horn-shaped chrome bumpers underneath the indicator lights, the Lusso ('luxury') did away with many of the electric additions to the GTE (including the window winders and the automatic overdrive), to push the performance closer to that expected of a Ferrari – 150mph and 0-60mph in eight seconds.

There is a footnote to the 250GTE story that marks the total refinement and separation of Ferrari road and racing cars. The last 50 were fitted with the new 4-litre Ferrari 330 engine and termed '330 America'. Sold only in the American market, they represent the total transformation of the Ferrari 250 from racer to GT. Today, the 250GTE makes for the lowest and cheapest rung on the 250 ladder, but no less than the complete Ferrari any of its racing cousins are. As testament to its abilities, Enzo Ferrari's personal road car was a 250GTE.

The 250GT Lusso was a wonderfully successful attempt to combine the raw thrills of the 250SWB racer with the long-distance touring refinements of the 250GTE in a stunning road car. (Courtesy David Hodges Collection)

1963-73: power meets the motorway age

The 1960s are seen by many as the Age d'Or of the GT car, and in most cases this is well and truly justified. GT cars went hand-in-hand with spectacular new supersonic jet-propelled air travel, the spirit of hedonism enjoyed by the fortunate few, and the glamorous locations of the jet set – the shining jewel in a particularly luscious crown. Motorways began stretching across continents. Starting with the precedent set by the German autobahnen, comprehensive and often unrestricted routes spanned Britain, America, France and Italy, paving the way for powerful GTs to ply their way to exotic locations, be they the boulevards of Monaco, the twisting reaches of the Futa Pass, the snowy climes of St Moritz or the open plains of Route 66. The 1960s and the GT go hand in hand.

IN ONE FELL SWOOP, THE CARS THAT HAD ONCE SEEMED SO ADVANCED BECAME UNDESIRABLE DINOSAURS.

The nature of a '60s GT car was far from merely being a question of image, however. Cars became easier and more rewarding to drive thanks to technology

Sixties GT motoring can be summed up by the Lamborghini Espada – power, luxury, classic looks and then-modern technology. (Courtesy David Hodges Collection)

Inset: The sixties were not all about the ultra-wealthy. Alfa Romeo spearheaded the affordable GT class with its Giulia GT range. (Courtesy Rick Clough)

The Gordon-Keeble was typical of many sixties European GT cars – Italianate lines, an American V8 engine, and an exclusive price tag. (Courtesy Roy Dowding)

gained in racing. They became more accessible too – the average and relative prices of the 1960s GT cars featured here easily undercuts the more exclusive 1950s. Before the fuel crisis year of 1974, manufacturers had no need to worry too much about fuel economy, so large V8 and V12 engines became the norm on most GTs to the point where a 'six' was deemed inadequate by many mainstays.

With this, power outputs climbed. Whilst 110mph represented respectable performance in the 1950s, by 1963 it was positively sluggish. Supercars such as the Lamborghini Miura and Ferrari Daytona recalibrated the scale of performance, making 160mph the new target. New firms sprang into existence with the sole intention of building GT cars: Iso, Avanti and Gordon-Keeble to name a few. Facel's practise of using stock American big-block V8s filtered through to the majority of GT practitioners, and the Americans themselves got in on the act, using their own unique takes on the form to produce some of the most striking cars of the era.

Technology also had its part to play in the GT experience. Unlike the highly experimental, part-time automotive sciences of the 1950s, advanced technology had, by the 1960s, become a wholesale operation. The basis for so much – mass-market four- and front-wheel drive, rear downforce, antilock braking, extensive electrical systems – can be traced to the 1960s GT boom.

Like all good things, the era ushered in during the 1960s could not last. The 1973 oil crisis brought the automotive hedonism to a dead halt, the following recession, shortages and lack of demand for big GTs put many companies into receivership and vanquished many others altogether. In one fell swoop, the cars that had once seemed so advanced became undesirable dinosaurs.

Today, however, the GT cars of the 1960s are coveted. Their purity of line – untarnished by the legislation and decadence of the 1970s – and the general optimism of the times infused itself within the cars, providing excellent driving experiences. Peacetime and a positive (in the early 1960s at least) economic climate brought the opportunity to produce GTs to so many firms that had lacked either the capital or the market: Mazda, Lotus, Citroën and Oldsmobile, to name a few, all developed innovations that would shape GT motoring in decades to come.

There is a phrase associated with the decade that 'if you remember the '60s you weren't there'. The long lasting classic GTs of the 1960s allow us to evoke the era and cash in on the glamour, even if some of us weren't there. Pop culture has a lot to answer for, but there are very few experiences more evocative than slotting an eight-track cartridge into a period player, firing up an impressive array of cowled instruments and guiding a practical time capsule somewhere dreamy and exotic with a leather-bound steering wheel.

Volvo P1800, 1800E, 1800S & 1800ES

Unlike any Volvo that had gone before, the P1800 GT car emerged very early in 1961 winning much praise for its Frua-sourced styling. Unlike Volvo's reputation of the 1970s and 1980s, in the 1950s and 1960s it was known for formidably tough rallying saloons and, in Europe, for the pretty little P1900 sports roadster. Never sexy, Volvo enjoyed an image of reliability and motorsport potential similar to Subaru's reputation in the 1990s and today.

The P1800 cast aside the compromise between aesthetics and performance. In terms of practicality, Volvo was onto a winner: the P1800 would inherit the B18 'Amazon' saloon's reputation for reliability and couple it to styling more suggestive of the Maseratis that Pietro Frua was working on at the time. The torque-laden, economical 1.8 Volvo engine had survived the likes of Alpine and Safari rallies, and could be relied on to endow the P1800 with enough high-speed staying-power to be useful in a grand touring role.

It even enjoyed high-profile glamour when, due to a refusal by Jaguar to provide television producers with cars for filming, a P1800 (actually owned by Roger Moore) was used for the purpose of international intrigue by the actor's Simon Templar character in the ITC series *The Saint*. Even today, a white Volvo P1800 doesn't look out of place alongside James Bond's Aston Martin and Emma Peel's Lotus Elan. Volvo had, completely by accident, become a 1960s media icon, a far cry from its image a scant ten years down the line.

Unfortunately for Volvo the cars suffered a number of problems in their early life. The first of the series, the P1800s, were actually assembled in component form by Jensen alongside the 541S and shipped back to the various markets to be sold. Not only was this process costly as time went on (it initially began as a cost-saving exercise), but it became clear to Volvo that Jensen was used to dealing with a different kind of GT, and as a result the quality was not all that was expected of mass production. Switching production to Sweden in 1964 on the back of 6000 P1800 sales, Volvo altered the specification too. The 1800S, as it was now called, ditched the 'curved chrome' theme on the bumpers and flanks in favour of sharp straight lines more in keeping with the times, and the radiator grille became a matt black plastic 'chip cutter' for weight and cost purposes. Alongside a more realistic price (the P1800 had competed with comparable Jaguars under the original pricing structure), the new 1800S, despite its name, had a 2-litre engine providing greater power and torque, making it more capable of keeping up with the rivals its looks aspired to catch.

SPECIFICATION
CYLINDERS = 4
CAPACITY (LITRES) = 1.8-2.0
POWER = 90-125BHP
TOP SPEED = 102-115MPH
TRANSMISSION = 4-SPEED MANUAL/3-SPEED AUTOMATIC
DESIGN = PIETRO FRUA, FRUA
BUILT = 1961-73

The handling, however, did not match the looks. Unlike the B-Series rallying saloons, the 1800s never enjoyed much in the way of chassis tweaks, making their handling rather prone to chronic understeer if pressed. If driven carefully, like a long-distance touring saloon, it more readily represented its role, and made for a comfortable cruiser. Weight, and a solid chassis, made for solid road holding all the same.

The final iteration of the long-running design was the 1800E of 1971. Putting out 125bhp from its 2-litre engine, it could reach a comfortable 115mph and stay there. The most interesting variant was the 1800ES, a stretched two-door sporting hatchback with a large luggage capacity that added to the 1800E's touring appeal whilst simultaneously deleting the rear fins from the ageing design, a shape that was revisited by Volvo's entry into the 'hot hatch' market in 1986 with the 480ES. In 1973, though, the 1800E was looking old, and Volvo, chasing sales in America, had embraced the reactionary safety culture that emerged during the fuel crisis, and found no place for the 1800E in its new line-up.

The 1800 series still makes for a sensible, value-for-money choice in classic GT motoring, with most examples made still

The Volvo 1800-series represents classic grand touring at its most practical. Here is Irv Gordon with his 1800S, the car that holds the world mileage record at 3 million miles. (Courtesy Volvo Cars Ltd)

on the road. An 1800 actually holds the world mileage record at 3 million miles, and they are as reliable as the marque's image suggests, even today. The only real flaw in the 1800-series design is its unsporting handling, but if that is respected there is no reason at all why an 1800 should not provide stylish grand touring for many years to come.

FIAT 2300S & Dino Coupé

FIAT – Fabricca Italia Automobili Torino – has always been a company dedicated to providing – on the whole – small, well-packaged family cars that handle with flair, and pack engines that respond to the thrashing of a keen driver. Good as drivers' cars in general, they are not necessarily refined, comfortable or powerful enough for grand touring.

Occasionally, however, Italy's least prestigious car manufacturer produces something surprising. One only has to remember the aero-engined Mephistopheles, the last road-going land speed record challenger, or any number of luxurious stretched limousines built as one-offs for FIAT chairmen to know that the flair is not just confined to the handling.

At the larger end of FIAT's engine range in the 1960s was a comparatively conservative selection of saloons comparable to Peugeots of the era. Solid, dependable, moderately fun to drive but not fantastically interesting. They were powered by a range of single-cam engines (this was before the days of the FIAT twin-cam, that favourite of enthusiasts) that provided reliability, but not always much by way of a sporting demeanour.

However, in 1961, FIAT entered into the GT market with a sublime coupé sporting a Ghia design not dissimilar to the Ferrari 250GTE of the period. Based on saloon mechanicals, the 2300S used the largest iteration of FIAT's four-cylinder, a 2.3-litre, for power. The oversquare block made up for the natural roughness of the lack of cylinders with plenty of torque, allowing the 2300S to cruise in three figures with many examples of exotica.

Always obscure, thanks to the natural predisposition of the GT-buying public for the equivalent Lancia, the 2300S was never properly developed alongside the saloons, and, despite its massive potential and understated image, a perceived lack of prestige kept it out of ubiquity, despite its excellent value for money (a fact that applies today).

FIAT's GT market saviour came from an unlikely source. Ferrari was eager to homologate its 2-litre 'Dino' (named after Enzo Ferrari's late son Alfredino) V6 engine for racing, but lacked the production capacity necessary for the 500 cars required, so turned to FIAT for help. FIAT obliged, and the 2-litre V6, not officially a Ferrari engine, found its way into 500 assorted Sergio Pininfarina-designed Dino 206GT mid-engined sports cars, FIAT

Dino 2000 Spider roadsters, and, thankfully for FIAT, a Bertone-designed two-plus-two coupé, sporting looks resembling the FIAT 124 family, whilst echoing Ferrari's range of fastback coupés. Today it is looked upon as a kind of scaled-down version of the Ferrari Daytona, and for what is essentially a licence-built Ferrari, offers greater value for money than any cars of the era carrying the Cavallino Rampante.

SPECIFICATION
CYLINDERS = 4/V6
CAPACITY (LITRES) = 2.3-2.4
POWER = 135-190BHP
TOP SPEED = 120-130MPH
TRANSMISSION = 5-SPEED MANUAL
DESIGN = GHIA/NUCCIO BERTONE, BERTONE
BUILT = 1961-73

The Dino range met with far more success than the 2300S, which FIAT, benefactor of such lucky coincidence, retired in favour of the Dino Coupé, whose race-inspired engine provided a genuine Ferrari driving experience and a shot of glamour for much less than the real thing. Galvanising its suave image, a Dino Coupé appeared in the 1969 classic *The Italian Job*, driven by a mafiosi portrayed by Raf Vallone.

Further development came from Ferrari. In an attempt to up the stakes on the track against the likes of Porsche and Lotus, Ferrari took on the Dino project officially, upping the capacity of the V6 to 2.4 litres and the resulting power to 190bhp. The engine was made available in the FIAT Dino too, making for an exotic 130mph GT capable of comparison with marques far above its perceived image.

We live in less snobbish times, but the years of badge-related derision coupled with Ferrari-like running costs has made the Dino Coupé one of the cheapest routes into 'real' Ferrari ownership (good cars appear for less than £10,000 nowadays), which, for a Bertone-designed, Ferrari-engined GT, is something of a miracle.

Clockwise from top: FIAT's 2300S took its styling cues from contemporary Maseratis and Ferraris, although it was a more natural rival to the Volvo P1800. (Courtesy David Hodges Collection); The Dino Coupé with its spiritual successor from the nineties – a 20-valve Turbo Coupé; The Dinos were treated to the same interior style as their Ferrari brethren. Pictured is the dashboard of a Pininfarina-styled Spider. (Courtesy Stuart Pugh)

Jaguar XKE ('E-type')

Born directly out of Jaguar's competition programme, the XKE, or 'E-type' (the car assumed the name after its popular usage, except in America) was the ultimate evolution of the Le Mans challengers, the XK120C ('C-type') and XKD ('D-type'), although William Lyons' mind was never taken from the road: the XKE also had to be a comfortable GT, capable of crossing continents with ease, as well as battling Ferraris on the track. In an almost accidental test of its grand touring prowess, Jaguar test driver Norman Dewis drove the new Jaguar non-stop from Coventry to Geneva, its 1961 motor show debut, when the exhibitors realised that there was no roadster for the display.

Malcolm Sayer designed the shape, derived from the aerodynamically inclined race-bred thinking at the time. Its smoothness left all other designs – including Ferrari – for dead. The purely sculptural shape of the Series 1 has been hailed as an example of modern art, and exhibited as such. In terms of pure design from this era, only the Citroën DS is comparable in its impact. Enzo Ferrari called it 'the most beautiful car ever made'.

Despite its price, the XKE is often compared to the Aston Martin DB4, the only British car to come close to its level of performance. The Jaguar represented probably the best value-for-money GT of its kind when new. 140-150mph for less than £2000 in the 1960s was staggering, bearing in mind that a

175mph Ferrari Daytona cost £10,000 in 1967, and was still considered fair value.

True to the name, the XKE used Jaguar's XK six-cylinder, initially in 3.8 configuration for early cars. These cars were the purest-looking variants, the two-door, two-seater roadster reaching the highest prices today, although their restricted legroom and shallow boot space limited their suitability for grand touring. Ironically, the greatest usability would come with the 2+2 variant of 1965, which is generally considered to be the least desirable variation on the theme, with its humped roofline, commanding the lowest prices today. In 1966 came the more

SPECIFICATION
CYLINDERS = 6/V12
CAPACITY (LITRES) = 3.8-5.3
POWER = 220-265BHP
TOP SPEED = 140-150MPH
TRANSMISSION = 4-SPEED MANUAL/3-SPEED AUTOMATIC
DESIGN = MALCOLM SAYER, IN-HOUSE JAGUAR
BUILT = 1961-75

77 RW, the first E-type roadster, gets attention wherever it goes. Note the covered headlights and unadorned grille.

powerful 4.2-litre engine, ensuring performance closer to the factory's claims.

It was America, Jaguar's biggest export market, that determined the fate of the XKE. Initially identical in specifications on both sides of the Atlantic, American legislation required the removal of the glass headlight covers and larger rear light clusters, along with de-smog gear stifling the performance to the point where many American enthusiasts replaced the aristocratic XK engine with the Ford Mustang's 302 V8 for the required performance.

In response, Jaguar reworked the XKE around the new Harry Mundy-designed 5.3-litre V12. Although it reclaimed the 150mph performance expected of the car and provided a configuration comparable to contemporary Ferraris, the V12 dictated a larger grille and flared wheelarches to cope with the more powerful running gear. The new V12 ate fuel too, often at a rate of less than ten miles per gallon, making it rather unpopular during the oil crisis, hurrying its departure in 1975 to be replaced with the equally anachronistic (yet more practical) XJS V12.

Today, XKEs can be split into two camps: the preened concours d'elegance roadsters and two-seat coupés often deemed too valuable to use regularly, and the less attractive, yet more useful 2+2 variants making for reasonably-priced practical classic Grand Tourers, probably their best role today, and there are endless specialists throughout the world dedicated to servicing and improving the usability of this car, the all-time favourite of many.

The later Series 3 E-type with its V12 engine courted controversy with its chrome grille, but many agree that the altered wheelarch treatment accommodates the wheels better than on the Series 1 and 2. Note the open headlights with their chrome-straked surrounds, introduced on the Series 2 to comply with American regulations.
(Courtesy David Hodges Collection)

Facel Vega Facel II

With the Facel Vega recipe firmly established with the FVS and HK500, it was not surprising when many rival manufacturers began to see the potential of 'stock' parts, and soon the HK500 was beginning to look dated. GT cars of the 1960s no longer had stately grilles and finned tails, but more racing-inspired aerodynamics and chiselled lines. Even the Bentleys that Facel intended to rival had become a very different breed since the HK500 met the R-Type Continental, evolving into heavy luxury barges, rather than capable GTs. In short, the Facel Vega was becoming seriously overshadowed in a market it once had cornered. Alongside the value-for-money Jaguar XKE, the HK500 looked like something of an anachronism.

The HK500 was overhauled to become the Vega Facel II in 1962. The first revision was to the braking – drum brakes had made the HK500 something of a handful in situations requiring a hasty halt – so, on the Facel II, Jaguar-style discs were employed on all four wheels. The distinctive Vega snout was narrowed to look more contemporary among leaner competitors like Aston Martins. The double-stacked headlights were faired over with glass, giving a similar appearance to contemporary Mercedes-Benz saloons. Other Mercedes-influenced features of the II included the trim roofline – this car was clearly more 'European' than the HK500, with its distinctly American-influenced lines, although certain Facel features, such as the dramatically sweeping wheel-arches and fluted tail-lights, remained.

The Facel II was certainly sharper to drive than its predecessor, thanks to the advances in technology embraced by the car. The engine, now only available as a 6.3-litre (unlike the raft of engine sizes available on the FVS) provided startling power delivery, incapable of catching a fire-breathing Ferrari but decently swift for taking in a derestricted European motorway at high-speed. Firmer suspension, coupled with the new brakes, made for improved handling with the emphasis on comfort, and the majority of Facel II customers opted for Chrysler Torqueflite automatic transmission giving 130mph on an available 355bhp. With a rare manual gearbox from Pont-a-mousson, the potential of the Chrysler big-block really showed. Available horsepower climbed to 390, giving 140mph performance and acceleration capable of reeling in an Aston Martin DB4. Only the weight of this big GT – over two tonnes – blunted its massive performance potential.

SPECIFICATION
CYLINDERS = V8
CAPACITY (LITRES) = 6.3
POWER = 355-390BHP
TOP SPEED = 130-140MPH
TRANSMISSION = 4-SPEED MANUAL/3-SPEED AUTOMATIC
DESIGN = JEAN DANINOS, FACEL
BUILT = 1962-64

The Facel II story was eventually brought to a rather ignominious end. The French fiscal laws did not really favour GT cars of the Vega's capacity, and Jean Daninos sought greater profits through the smaller, more modern sports convertible called the Facel Vega Facellia. Initially it used the 1.8-litre unit from the Volvo P1800, but questions about its reliability brought on massive warranty claims that threatened Facel's future. Daninos chose the expensive route to solve this problem by building his own engine for the car and renaming it the Facel III, but by this time the company debt was too great to continue car production, bringing an unfortunate end to this elegant GT company. It was the last true French GT until Citroën picked up the baton with the 1970 SM.

Today the Facel Vega Facel II is a highly exclusive prospect, commanding massive prices due to its rarity and superlative build quality. Although at the time it was looked down upon by purists due to the blue-collar origins of the engine, today it is something of a delicacy, and there really is very little like it. It represents the heart of this golden age of grand touring.

Alfa Romeo 2600 Sprint

Released in 1962, the Alfa Romeo 2600 range was wilfully different to the line-up it replaced. The 2000 range, with its 2-litre twin-cam 'four' basis was sporting to drive, but in a market increasingly interested in luxury and high torque reserves, the 2000 looked frequently out of its depth. Harking back to Alfa's vintage '6C' Grand Tourers, the 2600 added an extra two cylinders to the 2000 block, creating an extra 600cc for its straight-six, unusual for a company so readily associated with the V6 engine nowadays, but the 2600 Sprint Berlinetta was a Grand Tourer unlike any other Alfa Romeo in the line-up.

The 2600 range included a large luxury saloon, the 2600 Berlina, its styling clearly influenced by the smaller Giulietta cars, and a similar Spider convertible, with beautifully balanced lines that made it look like a scaled-up Giulietta Spider, and none the worse for it. The 2600 Sprint was, however, a bold visual experiment for Alfa Romeo. Styled by Bertone, it featured a low snout with four headlights, a semi-fastback profile with a truncated Kamm-tail for high-speed aerodynamic stability, and cleaner lines than the Spider and Berlina. The traditional triangular Alfa Romeo 'shield' sat uncomfortably in the middle of the full-width grille, an awkward but necessary concession to remind the public of the car's origins.

With the exception of the engine it was impossible to visually associate these cars. The intentions of Alfa were clear – it wanted to rival the British with a recipe virtually exclusively employed in Britain: straight-six engine, parts-bin basis and bespoke styling. The 2600 Spider lent its shortened Berlina floorplan and standard 5-speed manual gearbox – this car had the cuore sportivo of Alfa Romeo, and no automatic transmission would ever be available, which possibly goes some way to explaining the car's lack of appeal in North America. Thanks to the weight advantage over

The Alfa Romeo 2600 Sprint Coupé, with its four headlights and low, slat-like grille which would become car design's equivalent of architecture's 'international style'. (Courtesy Roy Dowding)

the saloon, the Sprint could manage 124mph, a high top speed in 1962, which put it in the same bracket as the Volvo P1800 and FIAT 2300S (Alfa did not become part of FIAT until 1985, so the companies were still rivals), although it could out-drag both of them, thanks to its advanced twin-cam layout running through six cylinders. It had no natural rival until its demise, when the Datsun 240Z was unleashed in 1969, although that was more of a sports car than a GT.

The car was no lightweight though; thanks largely to the saloon floorplan and the exquisitely appointed interior, the 2600 Sprint never had the sharper qualities of a comparable Giulietta. Despite its popularity with amateur racing drivers (presumably because it was surprisingly practical for a racer of its classification), the handling was never a positive feature, succumbing to terminal understeer if pushed hard.

Help was at hand – if only for the wealthy – in the form of Zagato's aerodynamics expert, Ercole Spada, who set to work on the 2600 Sprint Zagato, reducing the weight, improving the aerodynamics and stiffening the chassis. Despite such previous efforts as the Aston Martin DB4GT Zagato, Zagato had entered a new era of controversial styling and the 2600SZ was no exception: faired-in oblong headlights, a gaping re-approximation of the Alfa grille and a full fastback with a bubbled hatch complimenting the trademark 'double bubble' roof of Zagato made for challenging

SPECIFICATION
CYLINDERS = 6
CAPACITY (LITRES) = 2.6
POWER = 145BHP
TOP SPEED = 124MPH
TRANSMISSION = 5-SPEED MANUAL
DESIGN = NUCCIO BERTONE, BERTONE/ERCOLE SPADA,
ZAGATO
BUILT = 1962-69

visuals, although the effect was positive – 130mph and faster acceleration was achieved without altering the engine.

Slow sales killed the 2600 Sprint in the end, thanks largely to a design that was never properly developed by Alfa Romeo, although the styling was highly influential, shaping the likes of the Aston Martin DBS and countless BMWs throughout the 1960s and beyond. Today, the rare 2600 Sprint makes for something of a bargain for such a high-quality GT, but its abilities have to be respected under hard driving conditions. Due to its performance and rarity, the Zagato variant naturally commands higher prices, although its controversial appearance makes it less desirable than other Zagato designs of the period.

Bentley S3 & T1 Coupés, Rolls-Royce Silver Shadow Coupé & Corniche

By the early 1960s, the Bentley Continental, based on the 'Standard Steel' platform common to Bentley and Rolls-Royce, appeared a shadow of its former self. Modified considerably from John Blatchley's original sporting design and made from heavy steel (unusually for Rolls-Royce, part of a cost-saving measure), it was only available as a large luxury saloon as per the equivalent Rolls-Royce of the period, the days of the highly sporting, grand touring Bentley looked numbered.

A saviour arrived in the form of James Young, a Mulliner Park Ward coachbuilder, who designed the solution to Bentley and Rolls-Royce's decline: a crisp and elegant notchback coupé (with a convertible option) with smooth, modern flanks, clipped fins, slanted headlights and the grille standing tall. Instantly dating the Rolls-Royces alongside it, it was a highly exclusive and fantastically expensive prospect, even for the average Bentley customer, although highly enticing.

The most crucial aspect of the deign was that the bodywork was in aluminium, liberating the chassis of the unnecessary weight of the Rolls-Royce steel hull. This made for faster, more Bentley-like progress (120mph as opposed to the Rolls-Royce version's 110mph), with acceleration to match. Interestingly, the convertible became the more specified option, and is still the more desirable (and expensive). Exquisitely trimmed in the classic Bentley tradition, the S3 MPW (Mulliner Park Ward) Coupé regained the ground lost since the R-Type Continental.

The S3 MPW was discontinued when Rolls-Royce chose to answer its critics radically in 1965. The Rolls-Royce Silver Shadow series that replaced the Silver Cloud was a thoroughly modern design, utilising a monocoque construction, a concept that had overtaken the separate chassis in refinement terms since its sports car origins in Lotus designs of the 1950s. A Bentley saloon, the T1, was released alongside the Rolls-Royce, the distinction between the two restricted to badges and grilles. This marked the beginning of Bentley stagnation – only eight per cent of these cars sold were Bentleys. Due to the nature of monocoque construction, there was no provision for a coachbuilt coupé, but help was once again at hand.

SPECIFICATION
CYLINDERS = V8
CAPACITY (LITRES) = 6.2-6.75
POWER = 200BHP (EST)
TOP SPEED = 120MPH
TRANSMISSION = 4-SPEED AUTOMATIC
DESIGN = MULLINER PARK WARD/JAMES YOUNG
BUILT = 1962-81

While the Silver Shadow bodies – a mixture of steel and aluminium parts – were built at Oxford's Pressed Steel factory and assembled at the Rolls-Royce factory in Crewe, James Young offered a shortened coupé version of the Silver Shadow, a sharp-sided two-door saloon with a slightly shortened wheelbase giving improved handling (with the monocoque in place, the handling of the Silver Shadow and T1 saloons was leagues ahead of previous Rolls-Royce and Bentley models already).

Picking up James Young's baton, in 1966 Rolls-Royce started offering a Bentley T1 Coupé and Rolls-Royce equivalent. Available as two-door convertibles or coupés, Rolls-Royce's subsidiary coachbuilder Mulliner Park Ward fashioned an American-style 'Coke-bottle' design, with slightly bigger rear fins to accommodate the change. With a properly sorted shorter chassis, this model was better suited to personal use and grand touring. The advertising literature proclaimed it the "the strongest-built Rolls-Royce, that loves to be driven hard." Although never an overtly sporting car, the Coupé and Convertible capably tackled continental routes with a bias on strong traction. A Convertible can be seen doing plenty of European touring at the behest of Gabriele Ferzetti's character, Marc-Ange Draco, in the classic 007 film *On Her Majesty's Secret Service*, and among Steve McQueen's character Thomas Crown's extensive car collection in *The Thomas Crown Affair*.

By 1970, it became clear, through lack of demand, that punters did not appreciate what was essentially a badge-engineered Rolls-Royce standing in for their beloved Bentley Continental, and it was dropped from the listings (although still technically available on special order). In 1971, the Rolls-Royce Silver Shadow Coupé and Convertible variants were renamed 'Corniche', the Corniche Convertible enjoying a long and successful life as the pinnacle of Rolls-Royce open motoring, although the Corniche Coupé was discontinued in 1981, due to

The rakish lines of Mulliner Park Ward's Aston Martin-like 'S3' were initially controversial, but succeeded in introducing a younger clientele to Rolls-Royce and Bentley ownership. Peter Sellers owned one, and a convertible version appeared in the classic swinging sixties film Blow Up, *driven by David Hemming. (Courtesy David Hodges Collection)*

the almost identical specifications of the Rolls-Royce sister GT car of the time, the Camargue, which will be discussed later.

Today, the late 1950s James Young-styled Bentley S3 Coupé is as highly exclusive as it was then, and represents the expensive end of the classic Bentley market. The Silver Shadow-based cars, on the other hand, are probably the least expensive way into the world of grand touring Rolls-Royce style, although running costs are no less monumental. These were cars designed for the super-rich, and are a privilege to experience.

The elegant lines of the Corniche took inspiration from the S3, and was based on the Silver Shadow, itself something of a groundbreaker for Rolls-Royce and Bentley. (Courtesy Rolls-Royce Motors)

The ultra-luxurious interior belonged to a more decadent period. The convertible was in production well into the nineties. (Courtesy Rolls-Royce Motors)

Iso Rivolta, Grifo & Lele

Easily described as the Italian Facel Vega, Iso of Milan went from humble roots to stock-V8 powered GTs, only to disappear after twelve illustrious years, during which it perfected the GT. Each Iso was a work of Gran Turismo fine art.

Iso (pronounced 'eezo') was a contraction of Isothermos, a Milan-based refrigerator company owned by Renzo Rivolta. Ironically, given its later output, the first cars were licence-built Isetta 'bubble cars', as contracted by BMW to Heinkel and Trojan, among others. But Rivolta had his sights set higher – much higher. Upon the profits accrued from the bubble cars, he began construction of a high-class GT car. In 1962, the Iso Rivolta, named after the company owner, emerged from Milan.

Like the Facel Vega HK500 of the 1950s, there were hints of an American influence in the Rivolta, its aggressive nose curiously prophetic of the muscle cars yet to be released from Detroit throughout the 1960s. One of Giorgetto Giugiaro's earliest designs (he was still an apprentice at Bertone), it secured Giugiaro as a household name among the Italian Carozziera, his trademark cleanliness of line is still being employed today through his own design house, Italdesign. The sharp curve of the Rivolta's rear quarter-windows, and its notchback profile, went on to influence BMW's coupés, and their designer, Wilhelm Hoffmeister, after whom the window shape has been nicknamed the 'Hoffmeister kink'.

Rivolta chose a similarly large and powerful American V8 for his eponymous car, this time from Chevrolet. The 5.3-litre engine had no trouble at all propelling the Corvette sports car to race-winning speeds. In the heavier, yet infinitely more refined Iso Rivolta, it provided a smooth wave of power up to a top speed of 140mph, especially urgent when coupled with the Corvette's four-speed gearbox.

The Iso Rivolta was the first of a short-lived GT dynasty without equal, and one of Giorgetto Giugiaro's first designs.
(Courtesy M R De Vries)

Handling was, however, never a high priority, many road testers citing severe roll-angles and snap oversteer as particularly unpleasant details.

SPECIFICATION
CYLINDERS = V8
CAPACITY (LITRES) = 5.4-7.0
POWER = 300-390BHP
TOP SPEED = 140-170MPH
TRANSMISSION = 4/5-SPEED MANUAL/3-SPEED AUTOMATIC
DESIGN = GIORGETTO GIUGIARO, BERTONE
BUILT = 1962-74

To answer his critics, Rivolta teamed up with celebrated chassis engineer and racing-car constructor Giotto Bizzarini to devise an icon of grand touring: the Iso Grifo. Clothed in what is generally regarded to be Giugiaro's finest design, featuring a racing-specification Bizzarini chassis and released in 1963, the Grifo was available in the Rivolta's two states of tune, IR300 and IR340 – the numbers denoting power outputs. However, given the lower drag coefficient of the new body, and lesser weight, the Grifo could manage 150mph. Disc brakes all round meant that it could not only chase down a Ferrari 250GTE, but probably outbrake it as well.

Renzo Rivolta died in 1966, at the height of his success, and was replaced in his role by his son, Piero. Piero Rivolta had different ambitions for Iso, and immediately set about expanding the range with the Ghia-designed four-door Fidia luxury saloon. Built on an extended Rivolta floorplan, it had no natural rival beyond the Maserati Quattroporte, and later, the DeTomaso Deauville.

Piero Rivolta also sought even greater performance from the Grifo, in the face of competition from the Ferrari 365GTB/4 Daytona and Maserati Ghibli SS, but he wanted to retain with it the GT refinements of Iso. He switched to Ford 'Cleveland' engines in 7-litre, 390bhp states of tune (from the Ford Mustang GT500) for the Grifo 7 of 1968. A Targa model with a lift-out

Next in the Iso stable was the Grifo, said by many to be Giugiaro's finest design. (Courtesy David Hodges Collection)

roof panel joined the model lineup in 1969, instantly attracting the custom of John Lennon, who bought one at the London Motor Show. The Grifo also took on a more contemporary look, sporting pop-up headlights like its two main rivals, and, on the 7-litre, a large Detroit-style 'hood scoop'. Many believe these revisions spoil Giugiaro's original design.

By this time the original Iso Rivolta was looking seriously outdated, and in 1970, Bertone – and Giugiaro – were drafted in once again to pen a replacement. This time, the new four-seater GT, the Lele, owed much more in its looks to the Grifo 7, with

an aggressive squinting snout reminiscent of the Ferrari Daytona, yet with a dramatic swage line that ran through the doors and boomeranged back into the fastback roofline. Iso's fastest seller, it stayed, along with the Grifo and the Fidia, on the price lists until 1974, by which time one was in the ownership of Emerson Fittipaldi.

By this stage, Chevrolet was becoming angered by the use of arch-rival Ford's V8s alongside Chevrolets in Iso cars, and rejected Iso's custom in 1971. As a result, Ford 'Cleveland' V8s, this time in 5.3-litre configuration, replaced the Chevrolet 5.4 in standard

The last Iso coupé was the Lele, similar in style to the Lamborghini Jarama. (Courtesy Chris Harper)

In later years all Isos sported this menacing frontal styling with pop-up headlights. (Courtesy Chris Harper)

All Isos boasted an impressive sculpted interior typical of Italian supercars. (Courtesy M R De Vries)

Isos. This never affected performance, however, and buyers appreciated the wide spread of the Ford maintenance network. Today, either engine provides reliable, if thirsty, running, whereas contemporary Ferrari and Maserati models require frequent rebuilds for their handbuilt, race-specification engines.

The demise of Iso was a sad combination of over-ambition and international consequence. Firstly, Piero Rivolta attempted to enter Formula 1 racing in a deal with Frank Williams, which never came to fruition. Also, at great expense, a mid-engined supercar rival to the Lamborghini Miura, the Iso Varedo, was prepared as a one-off. Although its dramatic looks were prophetic in the design of such supercars as the Lamborghini Countach and Lotus Esprit, the prototype's handling was awful and the car remained an expensive one-off.

The final nail in the coffin for Iso was the 1973 oil crisis.

Killed by the fuel crisis and an unsuccessful stab at the Lamborghini Miura market with the Varedo, within ten years this badge had gone from gracing refrigerators and bubble cars to some of Maserati and Ferrari's closest rivals. (Courtesy M R De Vries)

Suddenly, American manufacturers started downsizing their engines and pulling out of limited-supply arrangements. Coupled with a sharp decline in the big GT market, the writing was on the wall for Iso. Despite an attempted revival with a new Grifo in 1991, designed by Marcello Gandini of Lamborghini fame, and devised by Piero Sala, Reeves Callaway and Gianpaolo Dallara from Piero Rivolta's funding, the Iso Grifo 90 remained a one-off. Iso ceased production of cars in 1975, when the last Lele rolled off the production lines. An ignominious demise of a great marque, but one that certainly left an indelible mark in the history of GT refinement, performance and presence.

Bristol 407, 408, 409, 410 and 411 series 1-5

The sheer proliferation of models emerging from Bristol – always a single-model company – over the course of fifteen years reflects the high levels of ongoing development inherent in such a small company staying afloat in the often treacherous sea of GT manufacture, especially when financial circumstances and market forces sank such companies as Facel and Iso so quickly.

Laying the groundwork for all future Bristols, the 407 used the tried and tested chassis from the previous Bristol, but this time fitted a big 5.2-litre Chrysler V8 in the style of Facel Vega

(still around, of course, in 1961). Unfortunately for Bristol, this installation forced some changes from the previously sporting and technology-driven, if underpowered, Bristol cars of the past.

Firstly, there was no manual transmission option, only Chrysler's standard Torqueflite automatic gearbox. Although probably the best of its type at that time (and for many years after – even Ferrari adopted it in the 1970s), its push-button configuration was probably the least sporting incarnation. Even so, the Bristol was now a serious contender in the GT performance stakes

The Bristol 407 (right), and early 411.
(Courtesy David Hodges Collection)

again, topping out at 122mph but beating Italian exotics to 60. Coil-spring suspension and a Marles worm-and-roller steering rack replaced the previous transverse leaf and rack-and-pinion development. It was required due to the weight and specifications of the new engine, but also made for rather stereotypically American behaviour through the corners. Still, this was an altogether new type of Bristol, not for the previous purist.

Externally, the 407 differed little from the 405/406 cars that preceded it, and consequently looked dated by 1964. Along with a slight change in suspension type to counter the criticisms aimed at the 407's handling, the 408 of 1964 was restyled, featuring a much broader grille incorporating driving lamps, and sharp little cutaways at the edges for the headlights, reminiscent of Sydney Enever's MG B-series. Power steering was standardised on all cars with the announcement of the 1965 409, followed by upgraded brakes. More suitable wheels for the chassis, a twin-circuit fluid system for the brakes and, at long last, a floor-mounted gear shifter made it onto 1968's 410.

It was the 411 of 1969 that was to see the final modifications of the Bristol design that would see it into the 1970s. Abandoning separate model names for series designations, Bristol boss Tony Crook systematically addressed each criticism that had been aimed at the 407-410 range. First the style was modernised to look less glitzy, with smaller fins and less chrome,

then, from the Series 2 of 1970, the improvements to ride and handling began, first with a self-levelling suspension system (in the American idiom rather than the French), and later with a serious work-over on the ageing chassis in its last incarnation in 1975 as the Series 5. Other improvements were either imposed or inspired by Chrysler, firstly with an expansion of the V8 to 6.2 litres in 1962, giving 130mph performance, and later with the Dodge Challenger R/T-specification 6.6-litre V8 turning in 140mph in the 1973 Series 4. Serious thrust and interactive handling was a trademark on all Bristol 411s. Peter Sellers owned a specially commissioned 407 with convertible coachwork, internally upgraded to 411 specifications.

The 411 Series 3 of 1972 shaped Bristols up to the present day with its modern styling. Somehow recalling a grille-less Alfa Romeo 2600 Sprint, the Bristol became squarer, sharper-edged and bluff-nosed, sporting big quad headlamps and very little brightwork to keep the car 'modern' for longer. Since the 411, the Bristol recipe has never really changed – understated looks, big V8, a pliant ride and handling – it provides its interpretation of the best type of Grand Tourer and delivers to a loyal following with an unswerving dedication to quality.

The final restyle of the 411 represents not only aerodynamic advances, but also the progressive trends in GT styling throughout the course of the sixties. It was not without its unique quirks though – that panel behind the front wheelarch beneath the chrome beltline swings up to reveal the spare wheel.
(Courtesy David Hodges Collection)

Jensen CV8 & Interceptor

Jensen's CV8 and Interceptor demonstrate the progressive changes in the company throughout the 1960s, from quintessentially British shoestring innovator with the 541 series, which really was showing its age by the early 1960s, to a purveyor of what many consider to sum up the GT genre – the Interceptor.

The CV8 followed the principles of the 541 – four seats clothed in an Eric Neale-designed fibreglass bodyshell, this time eschewing the 1950s curves and blisters for something far more aggressive and muscular. The looks were not in vain either, for under the bonnet lay not the old 4-litre Austin-derived straight-six, but a big V8 from Chrysler. Jensen's intentions were clear – it was chasing Bristol in the Anglo-American GT market. The 6.2-litre unit was far more suited to the Torqueflite automatic 3-speed transmission, also from Chrysler, and this was issued far more regularly than the optional 4-speed manual. Smooth and unruffled, the CV8 (Chrysler V-8) became highly respected in the GT-driving world.

In the 1960s, as today, fashion and marketing were fickle things. The 1960s was the most fertile period in terms of GT

The aggressive nose was a departure from tradition, and caused a degree of controversy. (Courtesy David Hodges Collection)

cars appearing on the market and Jensen struggled to promote its CV8 to a market seduced at one end by the value of a Jaguar XKE, and at the other by the thoroughbred glamour of an Aston Martin DB4. Whilst the CV8 was fast (130mph was an effortless target for a big engine in light bodywork), many GT buyers were suspicious of fibreglass and somewhat put off by the size of the company. Jensen never marketed the CV8 as widely as other, more mainstream companies (despite its supporting role in the TV series *The Baron*) and the styling, whilst distinctive and

modern, was not as cohesive as that of others – the severity of the slanted headlights, the odd shape of the grille and the strange

SPECIFICATION
CYLINDERS = V8
CAPACITY (LITRES) = 6.3-7.2
POWER = 330-375BHP
TOP SPEED = 130MPH
TRANSMISSION = 4-SPEED MANUAL, 3-SPEED AUTOMATIC
DESIGN = ERIC NEALE, JENSEN/ALFREDO VIGNALE, VIGNALE
BUILT = 1962-76, 1983-90

Opposite: The lines of the CV8 were evolved from the blistered features of the 541. (Courtesy David Hodges Collection)

aforementioned jet set, and could be seen cruising the boulevards of Monaco, or high in the mountains of St Moritz on deep-tread tires with skis strapped to the fastback roof. It captured the spirit of the times perfectly, although even in these pre-fuel crisis years, it was an expensive car to run – with such a big engine in such a heavy car (around two tonnes), miles per gallon were often below ten. Even so, Jensen offered a 375bhp SP version with the 7.2-litre V8 from the Dodge Charger 440 R/T muscle car. Top speed remained pretty much the same, although the 0-60mph time was even quicker – less than eight seconds, perfect for seeing away a little Renault or Simca on a trans-European autoroute. Jensen even expanded the range further with a convertible version which was, and still is, the most expensive and exclusive version, which sold well in America to the likes of Frank Sinatra. Jensen returned as technical pioneer with the four wheel drive FF version, although that is treated as a different car in this book.

In the end it was a mixture of recession and oil crisis that sank the Interceptor – it suddenly became a dinosaur of a car, and its market shrank overnight. Despite the intervention of Jensen's GT, a smaller car with similar abilities, it could never return Jensen to its heyday of the 1960s, and the company finally sank into receivership in 1976. However, a few more Interceptor 'Series 4' cars were completed at great expense between 1983 and 1990, as a rare and individualistic alternative to the Aston Martins of the era. Despite another revival in the late 1990s with a Ford V8-engined sports car called the SV8, the big Jensen Grand Tourer never returned. Nowadays, many Interceptors have suffered from rust and high fuel prices, high restoration costs and unrepresentative eventual values, but the correct modern fettling, alternative fuel technology and selective use means that many Interceptor owners are living that 1960s GT dream once again.

indentation across the back of the car, on which the lights were mounted, came in for criticism by aesthetes used to the smooth curves of a Jaguar, or the sharp-suited modernity of a Lancia.

In response, Jensen gave up on the P66, the fibreglass prototype it had in store to replace the CV8 and turned to Vignale to style it a newer, higher profile car that would tide the company over into the 1970s. Vignale styled a striking classic of the genre – squared-off lines, stern lights and grille and understated vents and bulges, topped off with a practical hatch and tough-looking alloy wheels outside, whilst inside, the sumptuous interior was fronted with a dashboard like Concorde – this was going to be very much a jet-setters' car.

Dubbed the 'Interceptor' – a bold statement of intent – it turned Jensen's fortunes around, though perhaps at the expense of its traditional technical innovations. The body was made of steel, automatic transmission was virtually standard, and labour-saving extras from American cars, such as remotely opening fuel filler caps and electric radio aerials became other standard fitments.

Unlike the CV8 it became a strong seller, especially with the

Alfa Romeo Giulia Sprint GT, GT Junior and GTV

Alfa Romeo's 105-Series Giulia Sprint GT, without a doubt, laid the groundwork for every 'affordable' GT that followed it. The choice of the enthusiast, it displayed great practicality and the credentials for everyday use – in fact, it would have been possible to use one as your only car – yet possessed a sophistication that made it a Grand Tourer, as opposed to the likes of the Ford Capri, an aspirer to the GT market but not blessed with the sheer abilities of the Alfa that made it both practical family transport and, in GTA form, the choice of circuit racers and rally drivers. Unlike the previous Giulietta SS, this Grand Tourer was mass-produced, affordable and aggressively marketed, a policy Alfa Romeo has stuck to ever since.

The first Giulia Sprint GT, released in 1962 but not available until 1963, followed the styling of the accompanying Giulia TI Berlina, with a low-browed front end, prominent shield-shaped grille, large single headlamps on either side, user-friendly two-plus-two seating and a low tail that completed a pleasing waistline, bestowing a subtle curve underneath the elegant side profile of the glasshouse.

Producing 106bhp and propelling the Sprint GT to 105mph, the high-revving 1.6-litre twin-cam engine made light work of the bodyshell, bringing 60 in twelve-and-a-half seconds, available through the manual gearbox feted for its slick operation in the Duetto Spider. Four speeds were standard, five were optional, although today the five-speed gearbox is the preferred option, and frequently retro-fitted to make the car more suitable for modern motoring.

As its popularity grew, the development of the car became more frequent. Firstly, Carozziera Touring offered a convertible version, the GTC, making a four-seat alternative to the Duetto Spider, although it was to become much more rare – only 1000 originals were completed, although many GTs will have had their roofs cut off to create GTC replicas at the expense of their handling stiffness.

But it was the Sprint GT's popularity with racing drivers, and its track preparation that spurred on the further development of the car. Firstly, the most desirable variant, the GTA (Gran Turismo Allegerita – 'lightweight') appeared, prepared by Autodelta, with a tuned version of the 1.6, a stripped-out interior and lighter weight body panels. This car was formidable on the racetracks and rally routes of Europe (and even against V8 muscle in America in the hands of individual enthusiast racers). 500 were built, and

SPECIFICATION
CYLINDERS = 4
CAPACITY (LITRES) = 1.3-2.0
POWER = 106-220BHP
TOP SPEED = 105-120MPH
TRANSMISSION = 4/5-SPEED MANUAL
DESIGN = GIORGETTO GIUGIARO, BERTONE/TOURING/ZAGATO
BUILT = 1962-77
INNOVATION = THE FIRST TRUE AFFORDABLE 'MASS MARKET' GT

The Alfa Romeo Giulia GT series leaned heavily on the Giulia Berlina for its mechanical basis. (Courtesy Stuart Pugh)

The elegant Bertone lines are timeless. (Courtesy Stuart Pugh)

A rare convertible Giulia GTC. (Courtesy Stuart Pugh)

many Sprint GTs are converted to GTA specification every year, now frequently with the Alfa Romeo 2-litre twin-spark engine from the 75, and even lighter fibreglass body panels. There was even an unruly supercharged version, the SA (Sovralimentato), producing 220bhp, but only ten were built.

Keeping an eye on affordability, Alfa Romeo broadened the range from 1966 onwards by splitting it into two model ranges, both capable of grand touring, but suited to a wider array of wallets. Firstly, the Giulia Sprint GT became the GTV (Gran Turismo Veloce – 'speed' model), with 109bhp from the 1.6 and a characteristic stepped arrangement at the front of the bonnet. Slotting below this was the GT Junior, a 1.3-litre variant, designed to be more affordable and, as its name suggested, introduce a younger clientele to the world of the GT. Whilst the GTV was bored out to 1.8 litres (misleadingly titled 1750 GTV) in 1967, then the final 2-litre incarnation in 1971, the GT Junior's abilities broadened too. Firstly, following the practises of the Giulietta SS a decade earlier, in 1968 a GTA version of the 1.3-litre Junior eked out more speed and acceleration by reducing the weight,

and by the time the 2-litre version of the GTV appeared, it had 'upgraded' to the old 1.6, effectively completing the circle.

In the last five years of its life, the Junior had attention lavished on it by Zagato. The coachbuilder saw the great potential of the lightweight, high-revving 1.3 and 1.6-litre blocks and produced a more modern equivalent of the Giulia SS, the Junior Z, featuring bodywork oddly predictive of the forthcoming Alfetta series, and featuring a wide transparent Perspex panel covering the whole front end, with the traditional Alfa Romeo shield shape cut into it as an air intake, rimmed with chrome. Alongside the GTA and GTC, the Junior Z is the most sought after, and commands prices of up to £11,000.

By 1976, the basic design was almost 15 years old, and the new Alfetta series produced a GT car in its line-up to replace the 105 series GT, but the enduring appeal of the 105 has continued today, to the extent where an industry has grown around it similar to the venerable MGB, with nearly all spares and panels available new or reconditioned. Despite an ongoing battle with rust, this GT car can be as useful today as it was in the 1960s.

Alvis TE21 & TF21

If ever there was a car that spoke volumes about certain stalwarts of the British motor industry's reluctance to recognise their shrinking market fortunes and take steps towards modernisation, the Alvis TE and TF would be it. The 1960s was a radical time for car design, in some way more so than previous decades, and the GT market was dividing dramatically. On one hand you had the sports GTs, hunkered down over crossplies, featuring low-drag shapes with minimalist, sculpted interiors and high-revving twin-cams and V-formation engines. On the other hand, the traditional 'upper crust' GT seemed to be in retreat, the survivors of the coachbuilt era resorting to ever heavier, plusher fitments.

Hamstrung awkwardly between the two was Alvis. Unable to raise the capital to fund a completely new model, it took it upon itself to 'modernise' a design firmly rooted in the 1950s. Single headlights were doubled up in the style of contemporary Mercedes-Benz in neat oval chrome plinths, intakes were lowered,

bumpers toughened, grilles tweaked and engines marginally modernised, but still there was no way an Alvis could be called a modern car.

Not all the traditionalism was lost by any means, of course. The 1960s is often portrayed as a time of widespread and radical social upheaval, but the Alvis TE21 was taken to the heart of Britain's conservative upper-middle class, which much appreciated similar values to an earlier Bentley in a car, but at a much lower price; the walnut dashboard, big bakelite steering wheel and enormous leather armchairs exuded a wonderful sense of occasion for people brought up in an era of austerity and

The stacked quad-headlights and lower stance mark the TE and TF21 Alvis apart from the TD 21. This is a TE21 convertible, from the time before the black headlight surrounds were introduced. (Courtesy Roy Dowding)

69

SPECIFICATION
CYLINDERS = 6
CAPACITY (LITRES) = 3.0
POWER = 130-150BHP
TOP SPEED = 110-120MPH
TRANSMISSION = 5-SPEED MANUAL/3-SPEED AUTOMATIC
DESIGN = PARK WARD
BUILT = 1963-67

utility. It captured the imagination of 'Little England' brilliantly, probably accompanied by a Rover P5 or a Vanden Plas Princess (two similarly-appointed saloon cars popular with the middle classes) as a second car. Extroverts opted for the convertible.

This traditionalism never prevented Alvis' attempts at some kind of modernisation, of course. Carried over from late TD21 Series IIs, an Aston Martin-style ZF five-speed manual was available, stretching the ageing straight-six just a little further on cross-country routes. Alongside this, the TE21 was available with an automatic gearbox, like the aspirational Bentley, and power steering (long overdue on the heavy steering rack) was available on the Alvis for the first time. Even so, the TE21's sales were dwindling by 1965 and the car was looking dated.

The resulting update, the TF21, was the T21 series' final flourish. Aggressively de-chromed headlights sat recessed moodily into black-finished housings, rear fins drooped a little further away from their 1950s origins, and suspension was lowered fractionally for improved handling. Bumpers sat low with aggressive over-riders, indicator clusters became smart square units, and the car even looked vaguely passable alongside an early Aston Martin DB4. The engine had been improved too

– three carburettors, 150bhp and the latest ZF gearbox meant that this car could make 120mph quite easily, with plenty of torque too.

Unfortunately for Alvis, the likes of the Aston Martin were the first flowering of new designs, while the TF21 was a slightly modernised version of a ten years old design with running gear even older. Alongside the likes of contemporary (and affordable) Jaguars, it looked almost wilfully old-fashioned, and, when Rover bought Alvis in 1967, it halted car production immediately and concentrated Alvis output on commercial and military vehicles.

THE WALNUT DASHBOARD, BIG BAKELITE STEERING WHEEL AND ENORMOUS LEATHER ARMCHAIRS EXUDED A WONDERFUL SENSE OF OCCASION FOR PEOPLE BROUGHT UP IN AN ERA OF AUSTERITY AND UTILITY.

Despite an attempted Alvis revival in 1969 with the P6BS mid-engined sports car, corporate mismanagement and rival products under the BMC concern killed it at prototype stage, and the Alvis name remains unused to this day, cruelly losing recognition as time goes by.

Luckily for the twenty-first century Alvis enthusiast, the rigours of building military vehicles means that the 21 series, in particular the best-of-the-breed TF21, are still solid, reliable and dependable, especially after restoration, and their current high prices reflect Alvis' original promises of the highest quality above all else.

Aston Martin DB5, DB6, DBS & AM Vantage

It is, perhaps, unfortunate that a particular car no more special than the others in its dynasty (and certainly not the best to drive) becomes regarded above the others for something so trivial as a film appearance, but the Aston Martin DB5 is just that. Merely an evolution of the previous DB4 Vantage it resembles directly, and not even blessed with a special GT or Zagato-bodied version, the DB5's appearance in the James Bond films *Goldfinger* (as previously stated, actually a DB4), *Thunderball* and *Goldeneye* cemented its image, especially in the Silver Birch colour scheme, as the ultimate gentleman's GT, associated with the glamour brought by Sean Connery and Pierce Brosnan's renditions of the part.

In reality, all the DB5 amounts to is a sixth series of DB4 – heavier, slightly better equipped, a few logical modifications to the engine and brakes, and unfortunately sixteen per cent heavier than the DB4 Vantage it was based on. The powerful DB4 Vantage unit was carried over on top-spec triple Weber carburettors, but the sheer weight of the DB5 steamrollered over the more overt sporting performance of the '4 Vantage, making the driving experience smoother, easier to control and more refined, but no quicker, although around 30lb/ft of torque more than the outgoing DB4 series made its cruising capabilities on the motorways more pronounced. The convertible option remained, and is one of the most sought after cars in the world today, commanding in the region of £120,000 for a good one.

Despite its success, partially off the back of the 007 films, Aston Martin developed the DB series further. The development began with the production of a few Volante convertibles, built on the short chassis of the DB5, but with a more aerodynamic 'Kamm-tail' at the rear featuring a recessed panel and a small raised lip spoiler inspired by the racing cars of the day; from the likes of Ferrari and Aston Martin's own DP114 racer. Gone were the now-anachronistic fins. The construction was different too. Whilst previously the DB5 had been built using the Superleggera method, attaching rolled aluminium panels to a heavy steel frame, for the Aston Martin Volante, the frame was pared back, and folds in the aluminium formed many of the structural points once held by the steel frame, making the same rigid effect much lighter.

This car, now termed the 'short chassis' Volante, lead directly to the development of the new Aston Martin, the DB6. Thoroughly modernised to look contemporary alongside the Jaguar XKE, the DB6 minimised the chrome bumpers, flowed the oil cooler grille into the radiator design, revised the rear three-quarter windows into a more rounded shape and retained the Kamm-tail of the Volante, and later featured flared wheelarches. Although many find the shape unappealing compared to the DB4, there is no doubting that it looks far more modern, and so much so that it was the shape that Aston Martin turned to when the DB range was revised in the 1990s. A longer, more accommodating chassis made the DB6 more usable and practical, and the smooth driving experience remained. The glamour hadn't gone either – Paul McCartney was probably the DB6's best-known driver.

SPECIFICATION
CYLINDERS = 6
CAPACITY (LITRES) = 4.0
POWER = 280BHP
TOP SPEED = 140-148MPH
TRANSMISSION = 5-SPEED MANUAL/3-SPEED AUTOMATIC
DESIGN = TOURING/WILLIAM TOWNS
BUILT = 1963-73

Although Borg-Warner automatic transmission was available, it didn't allow the fabulous twin-cam 'six' to perform to the best of its ability, and so carries a stigma noticeable by its price today. It may not be the best model to drive, but it certainly is the cheapest way into a classic DB 'shape' Aston Martin.

In 1964, Carozziera Touring displayed an Aston Martin concept based on a DB6, which revealed the futuristic nature of Italian design. David Brown chose not to adopt it as he did not believe the interior to be spacious enough, but accepted that change needed to occur in the DB series if Aston Martin was to survive the next wave of design trends (incidentally, the Touring design intrigued a tractor tycoon eager to break into the car business – his name was Ferrucio Lamborghini ...).

The DB6 represented the final evolution of Touring of Milan's Aston Martin designs, which began with the DB4. The faired-in headlights first appeared on the DB4 GT, and the Kamm-tail came about as a result of racing the experimental DP212 in the international GT class. (Courtesy David Hodges Collection)

Brown commissioned freelance designer William Towns to design a futuristic Aston Martin that would house a new V8 engine. Towns was a fan of American design, rather than Italian, and the resulting fastback design – intended to be one of a range including a Lagonda-badged four-door – possessed an angular aggression and potency reminiscent of one of Towns' favourite cars, the Chevrolet Camaro. It eventually housed the new V8 engine, but upon its inception it was fitted with the DB6 engine and christened DBS, and even made an appearance, following the success of the DB5, in the James Bond film *On Her Majesty's Secret Service*. Despite its excellent handling and unmatchable pedigree, the weight blunted the performance back down to DB5 levels, and, as a result, the 6-cylinder DBS is the cheapest way into an Aston Martin today, although the running costs should never be underestimated.

The Aston Martin V8 is another story in itself, and more part

William Towns' 1968 DBS was the final resting place of the Tadek Marek straight-six engine. Originally designed as a four-door Lagonda saloon, it was based around a heavily modified DB6 floorplan. (Courtesy David Hodges Collection)

of the 1970s GT scene than the 1960s, but there is a further footnote to the DBS story. When the V8 car was updated in its design in 1972, with a revised interior and nose treatment, despite the V8 option being the most popular, the 4-litre DB 'six' remained as an entry-level engine. This final resting place for the engine made for its most reliable, smoothest application yet, although the sort of performance seen in the more sporting of the DB series had been sacrificed for smoothness. Named the 'Aston Martin AM Vantage', perversely this machine is by far the cheapest and best value classic six-cylinder Aston Martin available today, although it remains something of a rarity, with only seventy-one produced.

Buick Riviera

Snobbery frequently casts the Grand Tourer as a purely European concept, with the leading centres for GT production being Britain, France, Germany and Italy, but this view is both blinkered and unfair, especially when the world's biggest market for GT cars is taken into consideration. Although Europe would claim to have the most hallowed grand touring routes, twisting through the Alps and soaring down autobahns, it is often forgotten that Americans make these kinds of long-distance journeys as a matter of necessity far more often, so it was only a matter of time before a US manufacturer delivered a unique kind of American car that not only suited this kind of touring, but was also acceptable in the highest echelons of European motoring too.

General Motors' styling supremo Bill Mitchell gave his motivation for the Buick Riviera as being a need for a car that

bridged the gap between Bentley and Ferrari. Alvis, in Britain, occupied a similar market at this same time – which only reinforces just how futuristic the Riviera was.

The groundwork for the Bentley comparisons was already there – the car was to be a flagship that slotted below the super-luxury contender (Cadillac) whilst retaining an element of sporting ability in terms of power, acceleration and handling. In the best Detroit tradition, it was fitted with luxury fitments from Cadillac.

SPECIFICATION
CYLINDERS = V8
CAPACITY (LITRES) = 6.6-7.4
POWER = 325-385BHP
TOP SPEED = 130MPH
TRANSMISSION = 2/3-SPEED AUTOMATIC
DESIGN = BILL MITCHELL, GENERAL MOTORS
BUILT = 1963-73
INNOVATION: THE FIRST MODERN AMERICAN GT CAR

The other ingredient in the recipe – the Ferrari aspect – came with the styling. Unlike comparable American cars, the Riviera's styling was sharp-lined, clean and futuristic inside and out, abandoning the fascination with corporate features like overbearing grilles, or the vain jet-age imagery that still clung onto American styling in some quarters. Amid the hordes of wallowing barges, the shark-nosed, quad-lighted Riviera forced other manufacturers to take notice of this Grand Tourer, as it represented an individualistic and optimistic future for America.

The car's interior was truly stunning, being both more comprehensive than American contemporaries, and drawing design inspiration from science fiction. Gone were strip speedometers, or even push-button automatic shifters – magnified gauges sat in cool steel-edged bowl-like pods on the dashboard, whilst controls for the stereo and air conditioning were integrated into a clean, intriguing arrangement of angular, intersecting

The first Buick Riviera came from a time when American car design was clean-lined, optimistic and forward-looking, and nothing encapsulated this spirit better than this first edition Riviera. (Courtesy Chris Knowles)

Motive power came from a General Motors big-block V8 – a unit also used in the Iso Grifo 7. (Courtesy Chris Knowles)

The dramatic arrow-shaped rear end of the third-generation Riviera. The fuel crisis forced a rethink of the Riviera concept and it was never the same afterwards – the 'boat-tail' was the last Riviera that could take its place alongside the likes of the Interceptor. (Courtesy Chris Knowles)

The 1968 restyle experimented with the aerodynamic advantages of a smoother prow and concealed headlights. (Courtesy Chris Knowles)

panels and lines. Not even Ferraris of the era felt so special inside.

Traditionalism prevailed underneath, however, on the perimeter-frame chassis. The venerable GM 'big block' 6.6-litre V8 (as seen on contemporary Isos) provided the power, driving the rear wheels through a reliable low/high ratio two-speed transmission and giving a top speed of 130mph, with muscle car acceleration. Despite the set-up, the Riviera handled reasonably well in comparison to the Lincoln Continental and Cadillac Eldorado.

General Motors did not leave the Riviera at that, though. In 1965, in an even more futuristic move, the headlights were altered so they were hidden behind vacuum-operated flaps, making for a more aerodynamic nose. The 6.6 V8 was bored out to 7 litres too, although by this time

the corporate influence was beginning to show through – GM had started using a Cadillac Eldorado chassis under the Riviera which, although stiffened for use under the Buick, exhibited more shortcomings in the handling department.

The final flowering of the Buick Riviera came in 1970, when it was restyled altogether, though no less appealingly so. This time, the side profile boasted a pinched waist and a 'Coke bottle' shape, kicking up dramatically towards the rear, while the front end bared its headlights once again, and almost certainly influenced BMWs of the 1970s. The most radical styling was reserved for the back end, where the rear

windscreen was funnelled into a dramatic arrow shape in the bodywork that ran through, between the turn signals into the bumpers. Fitted with GM's 7.4-litre 'Rocket' V8 and a 3-speed automatic gearbox, the Riviera's performance was certainly not compromised, although its demise came early – in 1973 the oil crisis struck, the Riviera downsized to a saloon-based 2-door, and the styling stagnated.

Even so, the original Buick Riviera remains the first true modern American Grand Tourer. It was used by such celebrities as Dusty Springfield and Robert Plant, and it still exudes a cool, subtle glamour even today. Its reliability (if not its thirst) ensures that the Riviera will be enjoyed by generations of travelling Americans (and lucky owners in the rest of the world) to come.

Maserati Sebring & Mistral

Eternally Italy's Aston Martin, Maserati sought to compete with the British firm's DB-series cars throughout the 1960s. Although the attempts at countering the DB4 with the 3500GT had been worthy, they had not produced the car that Maserati had hoped for in the international grand touring stakes, and development of the 3500GT was called for – a competitive theme between these two companies that would resume in the 1990s.

Instead of radically redesigning the 3500GT, Alfredo Vignale produced a crisp, quad-headlight update of the body, coupled with a slimmer grille that made the new Maserati – tentatively called the 3500GT IS – resemble Vignale's Lancias of the period. Featuring a 235bhp version of the 3500GT's 3.5-litre 'six', the IS was displayed on the 1963 show circuit to positive acclaim. In a move to distance the new car from its predecessor, Maserati introduced a new naming regime for the 1960s – using the names of international racing circuits that had seen great Maserati victories – and the car was christened 'Sebring', which had the added advantage of alluding to its grand touring nature.

The Sebring Series I met with reasonable success in 1963, but competition from Maserati's perpetual thorn in the side, Aston Martin and its new flagship 4-litre DB5, meant that the first 3.5-litre Sebring quickly seemed outpaced and outdated, and its 3500GT roots began to shine through (not least in the chassis).

Keeping one eye on the DB5 but realising the slight weight advantage over the Aston Martin, Giulio Alfieri, Maserati's great engineer, enlarged the 'six' to 3.7 litres, with a resulting increase in power to 245bhp. Despite these changes, it became clear to Maserati by 1964 that two options were available – match the Aston Martin's specifications like-for-like in an update of the Sebring, or use the new technologies of weight reduction and aerodynamics to completely redesign the car in the hope that it would keep the platform competitive.

Interestingly, both courses were followed. Upon the Sebring's release in 1963, designer Pietro Frua, on the Maserati stand at Turin, had exhibited a GT based on the 3500 called the 'Due Posti'. It was bodied in aluminium to keep the weight down, and featured many aerodynamic design cues that were becoming prevalent in the 1960s – a fastback roof, kamm-tail, faired headlights and a smaller air intake instead of a traditional radiator grille. Recognising the car's massive potential with the 3.7-litre unit, but keeping in mind the traditional clientele the Sebring had attracted worldwide, the 4-litre, Aston Martin DB5-equalling Sebring Series II entered production in 1964 alongside the new car, which was named 'Mistral', beginning another Maserati naming tradition – classical names for hot desert winds. The arrival of the Mistral allowed Maserati the chance to engineer a new convertible too, so the Mistral Spyder arrived at the same time, boasting an aerodynamically designed all-weather hardtop for retaining those GT comforts of the coupé.

SPECIFICATION
CYLINDERS = 6
CAPACITY (LITRES) = 3.5-4.0
POWER = 235-255BHP
TOP SPEED = 138-147MPH
TRANSMISSION = 5-SPEED MANUAL, 4/5-SPEED AUTOMATIC
DESIGN = GIOVANNI MICHELOTTI, VIGNALE/PIETRO FRUA, MAGGORIA
BUILT = 1963-69

The modernist Mistral immediately began to outsell the Sebring Series II almost twofold, and even Aston Martin was forced to re-think the construction of the new DB6 along the Mistral's lines. Maserati effortlessly introduced the 4-litre option to the Mistral in 1966, and although acceleration figures were never properly tested, it was probably one of the world's fastest GT cars at the time, with a top speed close to 150mph. Even the 3.7-litre version returned perfectly acceptable performance.

Both the Sebring and the Mistral bowed out in 1969, by which time, despite sales successes, it was evident that Maserati's

Opposite: The sharply-styled notchback Sebring was the conservative choice, but no less prestigious for it.
(Courtesy S Childs/EMAP Automotive)

The Mistral was the leaner, sportier, more avant-garde choice, its styling inspired by Ferrari and Jaguar, and copied by AC. Its profile inspired Giorgetto Giugiaro's Maserati 3200GT design of 1996. At one stage Maserati was going to reuse the Mistral name, too. (Courtesy David Hodges Collection)

future, like Aston Martin's, lay in larger, V8-powered cars. The Mexico, developed from the V8 Quattroporte saloon and 5000GT and Ghibli supercars, available since 1965, represented the new desires of the 'jet set' and made the Sebring and even the Mistral, with its advanced construction methods, seem outdated by comparison. Indeed in some ways they were, all being related to the 1950s 3500GT, and since the Citröen takeover in 1969, there was no place for old-fashioned approaches.

Nowadays, the Sebring and, in particular, the Mistral, are more practical propositions in the world of classic GT motoring. The Mistral especially, with its rust-resistant aluminium bodyshell (many features of which it shared with the remarkably similar Frua-designed British AC 428, which outlived it by a few years), is a bargain in comparison to the equivalent Aston Martin DB6, and easily its dynamic equal, although the rare and glamorous Spyder variant will always be worth premium money.

Maserati Mexico & Indy

Traditionally, Maserati had always been a sporting company, existing primarily for racing, funding itself through road going racing cars, usually specially-bodied for wealthy clients, and never really concentrating on road car production. Following a disastrous fire in 1957 that forced Maserati's withdrawal from competition, Maserati's racing bent looked like its undoing. Obviously, in the interests of survival, this had to change to reverse the company's flagging fortunes. It did, in 1958 with the 3500GT, but quietly, behind closed doors, Maserati was fusing the old ways of the racer with its new direction in (low) volume-produced Grand Tourers. Firstly, the 5000GT supercar emerged, sporting a Grand Prix 5-litre V8, a 3500GT chassis and wild handling, built for the Shah of Iran. Its tiny, 22-car production run and phenomenal power earned it infamy and alongside the Mercedes-Benz 300SL, it was a supercar before the phrase was coined for Lamborghini's Miura.

The 5000GT was too unrefined to be a true GT car, and the Shah soon commissioned a 4-door (Quattroporte) saloon version with a smaller, milder 4.2-litre V8. Maserati immediately put it into volume production in 1963, but the chance to mate the limousine-like comforts of the Quattroporte saloon to the race-car aspirations of the 5000GT was irresistible for Maserati, and the young Giovanni Michelotti, by this time working for Vignale and well-known for being able to design an automotive masterpiece within a day for marques as diverse as Ferrari and Triumph, was called upon to pen the new GT.

In 1965, the Mexico – named after one of the legendary Fangio's Grand Prix wins – successfully fused the sleekness of the 5000GT with the luxury and refinement of the Quattroporte. Bodied in steel and powered by a choice of Quattroporte 4.2 or enlarged 4.7-litre V8s, it soon became Maserati's GT flagship, its typically European elegance in the glasshouse and nose treatment finding favour amongst the GT-buying elite in Europe and America, especially traditionalists who might have found the Mistral's modernity off-putting.

Finding itself unrivalled (yet) by Aston Martin, and more refined and plush – if slower – than the closest V12 Ferraris, the Mexico continued pretty much unchanged. However, it was to be Maserati's rivalling of Ferrari, plus the new ownership

by Citroën, that ultimately numbered the days of the original Mexico.

SPECIFICATIONS
CYLINDERS = V8
CAPACITY (LITRES) = 4.2-4.9
POWER = 290-300BHP
TOP SPEED = 154-160MPH
TRANSMISSION = 5-SPEED MANUAL/3-SPEED AUTOMATIC
DESIGN = GIOVANNI MICHELOTTI, VIGNALE
BUILT = 1965-74

Firstly, in 1966, Maserati unveiled its Giorgetto Giugiaro-designed (Giugiaro was then working for Ghia) Ghibli supercar, a large, 2-seater sporting wedge aimed squarely at dethroning

The Maserati Mexico, the Sebring's replacement, at a motorshow in the sixties, ironically bearing some scars of heavy use. (Courtesy David Hodges Collection)

the Ferrari 275GTB/4. This streak of modernity running through Maserati (plus the success of the Mistral) meant that the stately Mexico was beginning to look stale.

Coupled to that, the Citröen purchase of Maserati in 1968 – and the French company's dedication to modernism and technology as seen in its DS saloon range – meant that the Mexico would have to be replaced in order for Maserati to stay ahead of the game. As a result, Vignale, inspired by the Ghibli, created the Indy (named once again for a Maserati victory in the Indianapolis 500), a similarly suave, futuristic wedge-shaped piece of design

that immediately rendered most of the competition in the GT world outdated once again.

Under the tutelage of Citröen, Maserati began to modernise its range swiftly. Firstly, in 1970, the Mexico was afforded electronic ignition. The Mexico was continued alongside the Indy for the same reason the Sebring was with the Mistral – traditionalism. However, it was in the Indy that the French influence first began to be felt.

Firstly, from 1971 a new 300 brake horsepower 4.9-litre V8 became the only engine available on the Indy (it retained

The Indy was the sleeker alternative designed to replace the Mistral, and took its styling cues from the Ghibli supercar – note the fastback shape and pop-up headlights. (Courtesy David Hodges Collection)

its ZF 5-speed manual gearbox with an optional 3-speed Borg-Warner automatic as an option). Then the Citroën engineers fitted their trademark hydropneumatic system. This pressure-balanced circuit of hydraulic tubes and reservoirs of air and fluid incorporated suspension and braking with unrivalled smoothness and complexity.

Mexico production eventually came to an end in 1972, with the Indy following in 1974. The French involvement had led to a complete modernisation within Maserati, and the confusing model line-up of old, traditional models and futuristic new ones had given way to a more rational system by the mid-1970s, with front- (Khamsin) and mid- (Bora) engined supercars, and front- (Kyalami) and mid- (Merak) engined GTs, by which time Maserati had been sold to Alejandro DeTomaso.

The two landmark models, Mexico and Indy, remain today as reminders of Maserati's turning point from traditionalism to futurism, and the 1960s GT market as a whole.

Interiors were as luxurious and comprehensive as ever. Note the row of dials angled towards the driver. Automatic transmission proved popular in the American market. (Courtesy David Hodges Collection)

Power came from two new V8 engines of 4.2 and 4.7 litre displacement. (Courtesy David Hodges Collection)

Studebaker Avanti, Avanti II & AAC Avanti

In terms of iconic twentieth century design, Raymond Loewy has cornered the market. It was his pen behind the Lucky Strike cigarette packet immortalised on screen by the likes of James Dean and Bruce Willis, and it was his seemingly age-resistant Coca-Cola bottle design that gave the design world one of its favourite phrases, the 'Coke-bottle curve', meaning a subtle, flowing dip in a car's side profile, like the ubiquitous bottle.

Loewy was already an established designer, having shaped the distinctive, aeronautically-inspired Studebaker range in the 1940s and 1950s, and was arguably the man who managed to integrate the tail-fin craze most successfully on the likes of the Packard Hawk. His eye for perfect proportions was unrivalled, and his Studebaker Starlight Commander is often cited as the main influence behind the Citroën DS.

Unfortunately, Studebaker's unique position in the American car-building dynasty was slipping by 1963. In the 1920s, it had been the world's largest car firm, eclipsing even Ford, but by the '60s, an age of corporations and conglomerates, this plucky independent was losing ground. It had to find a niche, and quickly.

The result was the Studebaker Avanti. It was intended as a pony car with refinement to rival Europe's best – in short, a GT. Built in fibreglass like the Corvette, its sleekness, trim European-style lines, quirky window treatments, subtle offset power bulge leading up to the driver's wheel, and lack of American styling clichés such as big chrome grilles and towering fins made it an instant design sensation. Alongside the contemporary Buick Riviera, America's automotive world seemed poised for an optimistic, modernist future.

It featured Studebaker's own 4.8-litre V8, which endowed it with impressive torque and the ability to take on the likes of the Mustang and Camaro in the performance stakes, but that was not its natural habitat. Its short wheelbase and taut suspension (compared to other American cars) made it much sharper through corners. In spirit, it was much more of a rival to GTs from BMW and Lancia than its American counterparts. In accordance with its sophisticated image, it was advanced for an American car of the early 1960s, with disc brakes all round and the sleek styling concealing a built-in roll bar.

Unfortunately, it arrived on the scene too late to save Studebaker, and the company sank a year later. General Motors bought up the rights to Studebaker, moving the company to Canada and, through its own economic assumptions, dropped the Avanti. The Studebaker company withered on the vine.

The Avanti, however, lived on, but not under GM control. For Avanti (a marque now as opposed to a model name) lives on as one of America's only remaining independents. The rights to the Avanti were bought by entrepreneurial Avanti fans (and ex-Studebaker dealers) Nathan Altman and Leo Newman, who purchased the old Studebaker factory in South Bend, Indiana, and started building the car as an exclusive, hand-finished GT, featuring GM V8s from the contemporary Pontiac Firebird, and a high price tag. The only real change made to Loewy's design was the use of square, rather than round headlights, for a slightly more modern look. The car was known simply as the Avanti II.

It remained in production – mostly using the Pontiac 4.9-litre V8 from the Firebird Trans-Am – unchanged until 1982, by which point the company was becoming too expensive for Altman and Newman to maintain. A deal with a wealthy customer, Stephen

SPECIFICATION
CYLINDERS = V8
CAPACITY (LITRES) = 4.8-5.7
POWER = 245BHP
TOP SPEED = 120-160MPH
TRANSMISSION = 5/6-SPEED MANUAL/4-SPEED AUTOMATIC
DESIGN = RAYMOND LOEWY
BUILT = 1963-PRESENT

Opposite: The distinctly un-American-looking Avanti, first unveiled in 1963 as a Studebaker. Note the rear, reminiscent of the Ferrari 330GTC, the grille-less, 'French' nose, and Loewy's Coke-bottle-inspired waistline.
(Courtesy David Hodges Collection)

Blake, ensured a future for Avanti, and the car was radically updated.

The new AAC (Avanti Auto Company) Avanti (no 'II') was aimed squarely at the European import GT market. Stripping it of chrome seemed to emphasise further the inherent futurism of the design. The chassis was overhauled to compete directly with the likes of the BMW 6-Series and the Jaguar XJS, making it a distinctly un-American feeling car to drive. The power plant remained patriotic though – the new 5-litre crossfire-injection GM V8. A convertible also became an option.

Throughout the 1980s and 1990s, Avanti seemed to swap ownership as often as the car was updated. Firstly it was bought by businessman Michael Kelly, who introduced a long wheelbase coupé and a supercharger to the Avanti range. Kelly then sold the company to his business partner John J Cafaro, who moved production to Youngstown, Ohio, and added a four-door saloon to the Avanti lineup. The four-door, however, proved to be Cafaro's undoing. It was expensive to build and no-one wanted it, and the company shut the doors at Youngstown in 1991.

The design icon could never die, of course. In 1998, Hot Rod garage owner Jim Bunting bought the rights to Avanti and set to work on a typically American range – coupé, convertible and targa – promptly reacquired by Michael Kelly once again a year later.

Avantis are currently built in a purpose-built factory in Villa Rica, Georgia. Modernised in style but still recognisably an Avanti, they represent the rare American GT car for the wealthy and discerning. A supercharged 5.7-litre V8 from the Corvette sits under the bonnet, propelling the design classic to supercar speeds. Loewy could never have foreseen such an amazing story for his car, which is surely the longest-production GT on the planet by now.

Gordon-Keeble GK1

In many ways a British equivalent to the American Studebaker Avanti, the Gordon-Keeble joined the fray as a fledgling company eager to capitalise on powerful and cheap American V8 engines and hand-built craftsmanship, only to fail in sales terms in a matter of years. Unlike the Avanti, however, there would be no philanthropic rescuer for the Gordon-Keeble.

The story begins with two ex-aircraft engineers, John Gordon and Jim Keeble, who shoehorned a Chevrolet Corvette engine into a Peerless – a British sports-special of the late 1950s. Immediately spotting the potential for massive performance from this 5.4-litre small block in a GT car, John Gordon designed a GT around it. 21-year-old Giorgetto Giugiaro, then working for Bertone and already amassing an enviable reputation as a prolific stylist and the natural successor to Giovanni Michelotti, designed an Italianate body for the car, then named the Gordon GT and bodied in steel.

In terms of looks,

although the car drew heavily on the contemporary Lancia Flaminia, it managed a brutish British tough elegance of its own: the headlights in an angular glare around an aggressively efficient grille, and a trim, elegant glasshouse and high waistline reminiscent of something more Germanic in origin.

The Gordon GT prototype was a sensation to drive and the motoring press raved. Acceleration was strong in any one of its four gears, and the savage torque of the Chevrolet engine rushed the car up to a 140mph top speed. However, on the business side, Gordon and Keeble were beginning to rationalise their creation.

A Gordon-Keeble IT (International Touring), the later model presided over by George Wansborough. Fibreglass bodywork and a fanatical owner's club ensure that these cars will survive indefinitely. (Courtesy Justin Wells)

Gordon-Keebles were made by an aircraft firm at an aerodrome and were always pitched at the jet set market. In many ways it was the model's success that led to the company's demise. (Courtesy Roy Dowding)

The prototype was fast but a little rough around the edges. The steering was unassisted and could be harsh at the limit, and although ride quality was commendable, the thunderous power of the Corvette V8 was less than relaxing in a British GT setting. Like the Corvette, Avanti and British Jensen CV8, the bodywork was changed to fibreglass for production cars, which lowered the weight and was also cheaper to mass-produce. The name of the company was changed to acknowledge Jim Keeble's contribution – Gordon-Keeble – and the car was ambitiously named the GK1, intended to be the first in a line of refinement and development.

Gordon-Keeble's aeronautical finesse extended beyond the quality of the engineering into the general finish of the car. Appealing massively to the jet set, the dashboard was modelled on the controls of a light aircraft of the period, festooned with gauges, switches and chrome levers, and finished to an exquisitely high standard. The V8 was eventually offered in a milder state of tune than was found in the prototype for the sake of smoothness (common practise in the 1960s as any journalist driving a prototype Jaguar E-type Press car at over 150mph would attest), and the Gordon-Keeble GK1 looked like it would mark the beginning of a successful and prosperous GT building regime.

Unfortunately for Gordon-Keeble, it was excess, rather than lack, of demand that sealed the demise of the company. It had envisaged humble beginnings and a good reputation, but its meticulous and laborious method of building these GTs made for a long and angry waiting list that eventually turned elsewhere. The factory – based at Eastleigh Airport in Southampton – simply wasn't big enough to cope with the demand, and neither Gordon nor Keeble were businessmen or investors with the capital to expand. New boss George Wansborough managed to sell 19

SPECIFICATION
CYLINDERS = V8
CAPACITY (LITRES) = 5.4
POWER = 300BHP
TOP SPEED = 135MPH
TRANSMISSION = 4-SPEED MANUAL
DESIGN = GIORGETTO GIUGIARO, BERTONE
BUILT = 1964-66

cars (appropriately renamed IT for 'International Touring') when he took over in 1966, on top of the 80 that had been sold in the two previous years, and the company simply could not sustain its existence any longer. The car was simply too labour intensive for the factory to cope with demand, and yet not commercial enough to compete with Jensen.

Today, this means that the Gordon-Keeble GK1 still makes an excellent car. Its obscurity keeps values down below the equivalent Aston Martin levels, but the sheer quality of its construction, its rust-free body, the aircraft-like balance of its chassis, and the simplicity and ubiquity of the Chevrolet small-block V8 make it almost practical. It is a superb grand touring device.

Reliant Scimitar

Although chronologically Reliant's Scimitar appears to be a cut-price version of more glamorous GT cars, riding on the coattails of the Gordon-Keeble GK1, its origins are somewhat more convoluted. For a car that began as a cheap Ford-based roadster made by a company more famous for the three-wheeled Regal and Robin, to its status as the Royal GT car of choice in Britain, the story of the Scimitar is an heroic one, especially considering that it very nearly remained just a concept for a company with no interest in putting it into production.

The story begins not with Reliant, but with luxury marque Daimler, whose sales as an independent car company were flagging, partially because of the SP250 'Dart', which, despite being an able sports car with a superb Edward Turner-designed compact 2.5-litre V8, suffered from several flaws (including doors which had a tendency to swing open on corners), and challenging looks.

A neat one-off coupé, based on the SP250 and called the SX250, built for Helena Rubenstein cosmetics chief Boris Porter, seemed to be the natural answer. Penned by David Ogle of Ogle Design, it oozed GT style, with low, quad-headlights, a sharp glasshouse and a bullet-like profile. Unfortunately, Daimler, never the most commercial of marques, decided against producing it, as it was seen as out of place amongst the range. The actual car, however, was superb, and whilst it was designed around a Daimler, it did not carry any of Daimler's trademarks, like the crinkle-cut chrome on the grille surround. Shortly after Daimler declined the Ogle car, the company was bought by Jaguar and became badge-engineered versions of Browns Lane products. The SP250 was seen as anachronistic alongside the E-type and swiftly removed from production. There would be no Daimler GT cars for another decade.

The 'Scimitar V6 Series 4B' instantly began attracting the 'old money' rather than the jet set, as it was rugged, unpretentious and understated.

Reliant, however, took up the task of producing the Ogle design. As a company with Ogle connections (Ogle's Tom Karen had styled its range of small cars), Reliant was interested in branching out to pastures new. Its Sabre Six sports car had much in common with the Daimler SP250, what with its fibreglass

Specification	
Cylinders	= 6/V6
Capacity (litres)	= 2.6-3.0
Power	= 87-135bhp
Top speed	= 117-121mph
Transmission	= 3-speed automatic/4-speed manual
Design	= David Ogle, Ogle
Built	= 1964-70

The Reliant Scimitar Coupé was a rugged and practical take on the Grand Tourer, which proved unexpectedly popular with the landed gentry, particularly HRH Prince Philip.
(Courtesy John Simpson)

Never intended for competition when new, the Scimitar has been used successfully as a rally car in recent years. (Courtesy Roy Dowding)

its makers would have wanted. Still, Reliant was impressed with its efforts as a GT builder.

Of course, Ford's progression dictated Reliant's. Whilst some of the suspension harshness was worked out of the ride, Ford's new 'Essex' 3-litre, 135bhp V6 engine was installed in the engine bay, making for cheap, low-maintenance motoring. The Borg-Warner transmissions were slick, and overdrive made cruising in top as effortless as GTs twice its price.

The 'Scimitar V6 Series 4B' instantly began attracting the 'old money' rather than the jet set, as it was rugged, unpretentious and understated, making it ideal for the aristocrat who wanted a sporting car with luxurious features which could weather being used and left on a country estate, and would be stylish enough for public engagements and continental touring.

The most notable of these owners was HRH Prince Philip, who commissioned Ogle Design to build him a special shooting-brake version. To do so, Ogle used mirrored Triplex glass to form an airy rear estate body that enhanced the car's practicality massively. The 'Triplex GTS' was delivered to the Prince in the late 1960s. Of course, the Triplex GTS spawned the production Scimitar GTE, but that is another story.

Its combination of ruggedness and long-lived mechanicals makes the Scimitar easy to live with today, although the earlier Zephyr-powered examples are rare and difficult to keep in tune compared to the later Essex V6 cars. Even so, the badge's lack of prestige has kept prices low for what is, in some circles, a highly regarded, impeccably pedigreed GT.

body, but it used a straight-six from a Ford Zephyr, an engine of comparable size to the Turner V8.

The production car was named Scimitar Series 4A (series 1 to 3 had been small Sabre sports cars), and was a mild success. It did everything expected of a GT car – cruised at high speeds, seated four in comfort, could carry a reasonable amount of luggage and had most options drivers appreciated. However, there were still some reservations. Firstly, the sports car-based chassis was hard-riding and slightly unrefined, and, also, the Ford Zephyr six-cylinder engine, whilst making light work of the fibreglass body, suffered from a low power output (only 87bhp in standard tune) and as such, cruising was not as unruffled as

Ferrari 330GT 2+2, 330GTC & 365GTC

In the field of visual appeal, Ferraris have rarely been controversial cars. Usually penned by a Pininfarina master stylist, they are more likely to be a masterclass in perfect proportions than courtiers of controversy, but with the 330GT 2+2, Tom Tjaarda produced an intriguing, visually challenging Ferrari design that divided the tifosi and proved that, from that moment, Ferrari truly had expanded into a world of exalted road cars far removed from the track.

As the long-awaited replacement for the 250GTE, a car Enzo Ferrari himself preferred to use on the road, the 330GT 2+2 had refinement placed much higher amongst its list of priorities. Although the 250GTE had been a refined racer, the 330 series took the road car operation much more seriously. Mike Parkes, at the time a Ferrari racing driver, was drafted in to oversee the ride and handling development to ensure that, although not completely removed from Ferrari's racing practises, it was pliant and forgiving enough for the grand touring enthusiast to use. The carburetion of the thoroughbred 4-litre V12 ensured smoothness above all else, and whilst it may not have been as blindingly quick off the line as Ferrari supercars such as the 250GT Lusso and 275GTB, it outpaced most of the opposition in a truly unruffled fashion, especially when compared to the contemporary trend for big-block American V8 power units.

And what of the looks? Whereas previous Ferrari designs had reflected either their track-bound rawness (an early Barchetta, for example) or their classical, flowing beauty (one only needs to think of the 250GTO), the 330GT 2+2 looked startlingly modern, with a sharp, high waistline, razor-edged air-extraction 'gills', a broad mouth of a grille and, most notably, four rather severe-looking headlights slanting sharply inwards from the straight outward edge of the bonnet, a styling feature which Tom Tjaarda would go on to make his own on such favourites as the Ferrari 365 California Spider and the DeTomaso Pantera.

Unusually for a Ferrari, its looks ensured its short life. Whilst later enthusiasts of the marque could forgive the controversial looks of the Testarossa and the Maranello for their electrifying driving experiences, this 'smooth' Ferrari in an era of rawness and pure glamour failed to win many hearts. Despite a mild restyling and a few tweaks for the 'series 2' of 1966, it was clear that it was losing Ferrari money.

SPECIFICATION
CYLINDERS = V12
CAPACITY (LITRES) = 4.0-4.4
POWER = 300-320BHP
TOP SPEED = 145-155MPH
TRANSMISSION = 4/5-SPEED MANUAL
DESIGN = TOM TJAARDA, PININFARINA
BUILT = 1964-70

Rather than merely replacing the unloved, if superb, 330GT 2+2, Ferrari decided to split the concept of road-bound Ferrari GT motoring into two ranges. Along with the 'series 2' in 1966 came the 330GTC and GTS (Coupé and Spider convertible), featuring much more traditional styling redolent of Ferrari's competition cars; and a second model, the larger and more decadent 365GT 2+2, a huge GT completely removed from the track, which is covered separately in this book. Beatle George Harrison was a 330GTC owner, as was Barbara Hutton, heiress to the Woolworth's fortune, who ordered one with the 365 engine, in a special shade of pink.

The 330GTC essentially kept the same underpinnings as its predecessor (production of which overlapped by a year), but featured a revised body which, as well as completely new frontal styling, shortened the glasshouse and severely restricted the rear accommodation, placing the emphasis more heavily on the driver (although the passenger seat was widened into a broader bench where, in the carefree seatbelt-less days of the 1960s, a child might possibly be carried between the driver and passenger). It was reasoned, evidently, that if you wanted a 'family' Ferrari, you bought a 365GT 2+2. The GTS convertible version ditched the rear seats altogether. A 5-speed gearbox stretched the touring legs of the car further.

The 365 engine caught up with the car, however, and its fitment in 1968 carried with it a huge boost in performance –

Ferrari's 330GTC represented a further separation of Ferrari's race and road car operations. This elegant profile also housed the Ferrari 365 engine for the first time in its roadgoing guise. (Courtesy David Hodges Collection)

155mph and 0-60mph in 6.3 seconds made the new 4.4-litre 365 GTC the fastest 'civilised' Ferrari yet. The Spider version, the 365GTS, commands the highest prices today on account of its perfect blend of glamour, luxury and useable speed.

By the end of the 1960s, however, it became evident that Ferrari needed to rationalise its model line, and the 'small' 365GTC and S were dropped in favour of the large GT 2+2, the uncompromising Daytona supercar, and the smaller, mid-engined Dino. However, the unprecedented changes of the 1970s would yield more Ferrari GT cars as the market reacted to crisis, luxury, and consumer demand.

Today, the 330GT 2+2 is a comparative bargain, as is the 330GTC when compared to the contemporary 275GTB; but the GTS versions always command the highest prices, as the glamour of roofless driving always seems to outweigh GT refinement in the world of Ferrari.

Oldsmobile Toronado

Europe has traditionally been the home of front-wheel drive (FWD). As a method of mass-producing powertrains and inserting them into entire car ranges, Europe has historically led the way in the mass-production of FWD cars. Unfortunately, more often than not, this has been responsible for creating dull, homogenised ranges of cars that, whilst they exhibit 'safe' driving styles and roomy interiors thanks to their compact mechanical packaging, are not the sort of underpinnings an enthusiast would want to find in his or her Grand Tourer.

It comes as a surprise, then, that the first true FWD GT of the modern era should not only come from America, but also be huge by European standards, in both the engine and body departments. The Oldsmobile Toronado does, in fact, make much more sense than this statement suggests, as it was an American company, Miller, which pioneered the use of FWD at the same time as the likes of Alvis in the 1920s, and another American company, Cord, pioneered its use on beautiful Art Deco era tourers such as the L29 Sportsman. The Toronado, therefore, was just updating an American tradition.

The engine was the General Motors 'Rocket', a 7-litre V8 also found in the Buick Riviera. The GM Hydramatic 3-speed automatic transmission ran alongside the engine, to the left, through a complex universal link. Despite all this weight in the nose, the weight distribution (largely due to the sheer mass of the car itself) was a commendable 55/45 front/rear.

It captivated in its looks too, which for the time were utterly otherworldly. The mid-1960s was a time when American styling was glassy and clean-cut at best, but the Toronado not only aped the best European influences, it added American science fiction optimism to the blend too. A knife-like profile, coupled with a long fastback that ran straight into a truncated Kamm-tail at the rear complimented a clean, wide grille and pop-up headlights at the front. Overall, it's hard to believe this car's design didn't in some way influence Ferrari's own Daytona and 365GTC/4, which share many design cues.

*The Oldsmobile Toronado pre-dated the Citroën SM as a large-engined, front-wheel drive GT by five years, and the first generation possessed inspirational styling.
(Courtesy Kris Trexler)*

The style continued on the inside, with a speedometer where numbers revolved around a stationary needle – another design feature copied by Citroën five years later on the GS. (Courtesy Kris Trexler)

Later generations of Toronado were styled more along the lines of muscle cars like the Dodge Charger. (Author's collection)

SPECIFICATION
CYLINDERS = V8
CAPACITY (LITRES) = 7.0-7.5
POWER = 365-385BHP
TOP SPEED = 130MPH
TRANSMISSION = 3-SPEED AUTOMATIC
DESIGN = BILL MITCHELL, GENERAL MOTORS
BUILT = 1966-71
INNOVATION: THE FIRST FRONT-WHEEL DRIVE GT CAR

On the road, however, the Toronado was a revelation. Rather than the power steering detracting from the feel of undriven front wheels, it allowed the driver to direct the FWD power through the bends quite unlike most big American cars, even the Buick Riviera. Unlike the 'muscle cars' of the time, it did not suffer from uneven ride quality either.

Unfortunately, the Toronado was perhaps simply too good for corporate America. It didn't sell as well as its rivals, and Oldsmobile perhaps thought that, rather than let the car be an utterly unique Grand Tourer, it should be a muscle car. In 1968, therefore, it was subject to a facelift that endowed it with a menacing front grille, a vinyl roof, and an elongated notchback in place of the fastback. Suspension was stiffened, and a truly enormous 7.5-litre incarnation of the 'Rocket' V8 became an option. Power grew to 385bhp, although the sharp driving characteristics remained.

The Toronado, unfortunately, didn't satisfy the muscle car crowd either, who preferred smoking rear tyres, and not necessarily such immense size and weight, all with a certain unsophisticated charm. It only existed in such a guise until 1970, when a further restyle made a bid for the Lincoln market, with exposed headlamps, plenty of ornamental chrome and a huge radiator grille. Suspension now became softer again, although it was still recognisably a Toronado by its driving experience.

Unfortunately, once again, General Motors decided the car's individualism made it somewhat unsaleable, but allowed the FWD technology to live on under the next generation of Cadillac Eldorados. Unfortunately, the suspension and chassis of the Cadillac squandered the driveline with its wallowing gait, whilst the Toronado became just another big American car, even if it did have FWD. As such, it is only really the 1966-71 Oldsmobile Toronados that are considered the great Grand Tourers. It would be a full five years before Citroën released the definitive European FWD GT, the SM.

Today, the Oldsmobile Toronado's relative mass-production, coupled with the excessive fuel consumption of the huge (if very reliable) V8 engines, makes them an absolute bargain for such an innovation in grand touring. Unfortunately for non-American enthusiasts, they are rare outside of their native country.

BMW CS

Originally introduced as a GT sister to the top of the range neue klasse 2000ti saloon in 1965, who would have thought that BMW's coupé would go on not only to iconic status in the European Touring Car Championships (ETCC), but would also cement BMW's reputation as a company that refused, flatly, to make a car that was bad to drive.

The 2000ti was itself a bold step forward for BMW, which had been struggling throughout the 1950s juggling fabulous Goertz-styled expensive creations such as the 503 and 507 with meagre Isetta bubble cars and unexciting and bland rear-engined saloons such as the 700. Buoyed partially by the profits made by licensing out the design of the Isetta, but primarily by the desire to cement a reputation to rival Rover and Alfa Romeo, the new saloons introduced a lively front-engined, rear-wheel drive platform with an emphasis on satisfying handling, an ethic that has underpinned every BMW since.

The 2000CS was a pretty, Michelotti-styled, resolutely European GT car. Using the 2-litre straight-four block from the ti on the same floorplan, but with a luxurious wood-trimmed interior coupled with the lightweight coupé body, the CS was born. Bristling with intriguing features, such as curious headlamp lenses that looped from the reverse-raked prow of the bonnet, and very tall BMW 'kidneys', and a timelessly elegant and modernist glassiness about the whole thing, a design classic emerged.

Such is the nature of German engineering, however, that the 2000CS could not remain in its original, undeveloped guise for long. The 2-litre engine was underpowered, and despite the attractiveness of the Michelotti styling, BMW had begun an aggressive corporate strategy with the new 2002 series, and the 2000CS struggled to fit in.

Enter the 3.0CS. Extensive work to the drivetrain allowed BMW to take the original up a notch by installing the engine from its new executive 2.8 and 3.0 saloons, rather than the family-orientated 2000ti. The new car struck a much greater chord than the 2000CS, with its smooth, torquey power delivery, exemplary driving style and bold Wilhelm Hoffmeister corporate styling, it oozed refined aggression and latent ability.

Still, 1971 marked a sea change in BMW's approach to its GT. First, the

The first in BMW's CS dynasty was the 2000CS, a Michelotti/Hoffmeister collaboration, which ushered in a new sharp-lined glassiness for European car styling.
(Courtesy David Hodges Collection)

The later Hoffmeister-styled coupé came with a choice of 2.5, 2.8 and 3.0 straight-sixes. All were thoroughly-engineered, solidly-built and expensive, and placed the driving experience above luxury features. (Courtesy David Hodges Collection)

2800CS, the base model with the engine from the 2.8 saloon, was dropped. All models now sported 3-litre engines, with the option of Bosch K-Jetronic fuel injection (CSI), and also of an automatic gearbox to broaden its appeal (CSA). The fuel-injected 3-litre engine now pumped out 200bhp.

Secondly, BMW decided to take the car racing. Bored out to 3003cc for a little extra torque, it wasn't necessarily power that made the CSL (Lightweight) so effective, but aerodynamics and a 400lb weight reduction. The racing version had lowered suspension, a wider track, Perspex side windows, a Spartan interior, non-reclining Scheel bucket seats, aluminium panels, and, most notably, specially developed aerodynamic addenda that earned the car its nickname, the 'Batmobile'. To keep such a lightweight car on the track, a deep front air dam, a tall rear

spoiler, and a roof-mounted aerofoil made it devastatingly effective. In the ETC Group 2 championships from 1972 to 1974, it was utterly dominant.

Still, the 3.0CSL was not the ultimate variant. The rise of Porsche on the ETC Group 2 racing scene forced BMW to develop the car further, and the engine was bored out to 3.2 litres on a par with the new G-series 911s. An enormous two-tier rear wing and 'splitters' on the front wings signalled the 3.2CSL's potent intent within.

Ironically, the other end of the CS range for 1974 was the 2.5CS, with 150bhp and a reduced number of options. It was a way of shifting the last 844 bodyshells. The car was now ten years old, and its limitations as a road car were beginning to show in its four-speed gearbox and a certain lack of punch compared

The CSL, in 3.0 and 3.2-litre guises with spoiler, wing, aerofoil, air dam and splitters, was the competition version that demolished the opposition in the German touring car race series. The roadgoing version cost more than an Aston Martin, or two V12 Jaguar E-types. (Courtesy David Hodges Collection)

to other prestige rivals. The fuel crisis welcomed lighter, more torque-biased cars and, by 1975, the noble BMW CS range was, unfortunately, a dinosaur. It was replaced by the more modern 6-Series range in 1976.

Nowadays, however, the typically European, square-jawed styling, perfect proportions and elegant simplicity, coupled with excellent build quality, make the BMW CS an enticing prospect, although rust and high parts prices can be a problem with lesser, less sought after variants. A good one, however, will always be a great classic Grand Tourer.

SPECIFICATION
CYLINDERS = 4/6
CAPACITY (LITRES) = 2.0-3.2
POWER = 120-200BHP
TOP SPEED = 105-134MPH
TRANSMISSION = 4-SPEED MANUAL/3-SPEED AUTOMATIC
DESIGN = GIOVANNI MICHELOTTI, MICHELOTTI/WILHELM HOFFMEISTER, BMW IN-HOUSE
BUILT = 1965-75

Lamborghini 400GT & Islero

Every now and then, a particular visionary takes a glance at the established status quo of the car world and decides that they can do better; one example is the Land Rover designed by Maurice Wilkes, who was let down by his Jeep. Horacio Pagani decided, in the late 1990s, that the Lamborghini supercars he had presided over just weren't extreme enough and built his own, the outlandish Zonda. History was made.

Ferrucio Lamborghini, on the other hand, was a millionaire tractor tycoon who was dissatisfied with his Ferrari. He thought it badly made, not fast enough and all together not the GT car he wanted. So he set about devising his own rival to Ferrari.

Lamborghini commissioned the best in the business to create a prototype – Salisbury diff, ZF steering rack, Girling disc brakes and a chassis devised by Giotto Bizzarini (of Iso fame and later his own marque), and Giampaolo Dallara (later to devise the chassis for such supercars as the DeTomaso Pantera and Lamborghini's Miura and Countach). The five-speed gearbox was of Lamborghini's own manufacture and Ferrucio's own request – the awkwardness of his Ferrari's gearbox irked him most about the driving experience.

The prototype, equipped with a 3.5-litre V12, also of Lamborghini's own manufacture, emerged in 1964 with styling by Touring of Milan and bodied in alloy in Aston Martin-style superleggera. Called the '350GTV', it was welcomed with intrigue by GT fans, but the whole operation seemed low-key and shrouded in mystery to industry onlookers. The production version, called '350GT', emerged later in the year. The driving experience was more explosive than the equivalent Ferrari, the 330, the gearbox especially was easier to hustle through the gate, and the light alloy body let it hit 150mph.

But it was still not good enough for Ferrucio Lamborghini, who sought greater GT comforts and even more urge than the Ferrari

Specification
Cylinders = V12
Capacity (litres) = 4.0
Power = 280bhp
Top speed = 156-160mph
Transmission = 5-speed manual
Design = Touring
Built = 1966-69

The Lamborghini legend began with the 350/400-series, its first 2+2 GT car being the 400GT seen here, with which founder Ferrucio Lamborghini sought to redress the flaws that irked him when driving his Ferrari. (Courtesy David Hodges Collection)

(a theme that would re-emerge when the two firms competed in the mid-engined supercar market). Only 120 350GTs were sold before the V12 was bored out to 4 litres. However, in order to economise slightly, the bodyshell was now crafted in steel. With the 400GT, two rear seats were offered as an option, making it even more of a proper GT.

However, even with the greater versatility, the 400GT was not nearly as popular in comparison to Ferrari as Lamborghini had hoped. The heavy weight (2862lb) blunted the 4-litre V12's potential. Also, the styling, although conventionally attractive, lacked a certain identity, hinting a little of Ferrari and Maserati from the rear, and perhaps Porsche from the front. It certainly carried none of the outlandish drama associated with Lamborghini cars since.

Lamborghini relaunched the car as the Islero 400GT. This time, the car only came as a two-plus-two. The styling became more pronounced, with sharper, more modern, flatter lines, squarer tail, a BMW-inspired glasshouse and a low snout sporting slimmer bumpers, less chrome, and the pop-up headlights that would characterise Lamborghinis in the future. Bodied in alloy again, the lighter weight and more aerodynamic styling unleashed the full 280bhp potential of the 4-litre V12, launching the car to a top speed of 160mph. The 'S' version got to 60mph in 6.2 seconds.

The Lamborghini Islero was an impressive GT car, but by 1968, Lamborghini was already well known for the astonishing Miura, a pattern that would emerge later alongside the outlandish supercars Lamborghini became synonymous with over the years.

It became obvious that a Lamborghini GT would have to be truly outlandish in order to succeed. The Espada filled that role aptly alongside the Islero, and later the Jarama provided a more conservative GT for followers of the original Lamborghinis.

However, the Islero faded into the background after two years when it became obvious to the car-minded public that Lamborghini stood for dramatic modernism and outlandishness, rather than Ferrari-rivalling conservatism, despite a spot of screen glamour, driven by Roger Moore in *The Man Who Haunted Himself*.

The Islero, and the 350/400GT line that preceded it have, however, passed into GT lore as the cars that took the classic Ferrari recipe and decided to improve on it, and their price nowadays reflects this. The Islero represents the entry level in the original Lamborghini market, the 400GT its height, but their comparative rarity, and associated running costs should not be underestimated. They remain, however, undisputed delicacies of the GT art form, bespoke and thoroughbred in every way.

Mazda 110S Cosmo

Unashamedly inspired by the Ferrari 500 Superfast, with its shark-like gills nestling between strakes running off elegant wheelarches, deeply-cowled headlights, rear lights neatly split by rear bumpers and panoramically-curved rear window, the beautiful Mazda 110S Cosmo emerged in 1966 to a bemused automotive world, but not only for its styling. The car not only intrigued from the outside, but also from within.

The Mazda featured a twin-rotary Wankel engine. German firm NSU had run into perpetual problems with the Wankel unit in its RO80 saloon, as it wore out the tips of its rotors too quickly, flooding the engine with fuel and immobilising the car, making engine replacement the only option. NSU was eventually bankrupted by these engine warranty claims and forced into the hands of Audi, which dispensed with it.

It was a shame, as the rotary engine offered so much to the builder of a Grand Tourer. Instead of conventionally igniting fuel by sparkplugs instigating strokes of the pistons, a rotary engine features triangular rotors within a sealed unit, forced around by a cycle of constant combustion, meaning an uninterrupted turbine-like surge of acceleration and completely unruffled high-speed cruising. The drawbacks included, obviously, the potential for rotor tip wear, and huge fuel consumption for the size of engine. Although the equivalent of two litres in capacity, the Cosmo's fuel consumption was closer to something with over four.

Mazda tamed the unit by strengthening the rotor tips and featuring fewer, larger, fuel-input ports, increasing torque and thus reducing the high-pressure wear on the rotors. Mechanically, the car was classic sporting GT – only available as a structurally rigid coupé, DeDion independent front suspension (though a live rear axle kept the drivetrain refreshingly simple), and stiff springs made for taut, snappy handling.

The power and speed, however, did not match the Cosmo's rivals for its price. The Cosmo was more expensive than a Jaguar XKE, and yet it only offered 110bhp, 116mph and a four-speed gearbox, partially redeemed by the smoothness of acceleration afforded by the nature of the Wankel rotary engine. Even so, the mistrust of NSU's disasters with the unit, and Mazda's constant minor tweaking of its engines, kept sales down.

Mazda responded to the criticisms of the lack of power and speed for the price with the 128B Cosmo of 1968. Lengthening the wheelbase allowed for more cabin space too, and the new 5-speed gearbox lengthened the legs of the new 128bhp engine, bringing the top speed up to a more competitive 125mph.

Still, the car was simply too unconventional for most European and American mass markets, and in 1972 the Cosmo name made its way onto Japanese domestic-market saloons, rather than exotic GTs, where it remains today. The rotary unit, however, captured the hearts of sports car enthusiasts in the 1978

Opposite: The Ferrari-inspired Mazda Cosmo was aimed at the Jaguar E-type market, but mistrust over the rotary engine, a high price and a lack of power compared to some of its rivals meant that it was always a rare prospect outside of Japan. (Courtesy EMAP Automotive archive)

SPECIFICATION
CYLINDERS = 2-ROTOR
CAPACITY (LITRES) = 2.0 (OPTIMAL)
POWER = 110-128BHP
TOP SPEED = 116-125MPH
TRANSMISSION = 4/5-SPEED MANUAL
DESIGN = MAZDA IN-HOUSE
BUILT = 1966-72
INNOVATION = TAMED THE WANKEL ROTARY ENGINE IN A CONSUMMATE GT

RX-7 sports car. Mazda did not return to the GT market until the 21st century with its similarly groundbreaking RX-8 GT car.

With little over a thousand 110S and 128B Cosmos made over its seven years in production, it makes a rare find. However, its relative obscurity keeps prices down, and the typical Japanese reliability of the rotary unit makes it a dependable GT car, although the thirst shouldn't be underestimated. It is a truly individual and uniquely beautiful car, and prices will eventually go up as they become more coveted by aficionados of the genre.

Gilbern Genie & Invader

Gilbern, the Welsh marque with a name derived from those of Welsh butcher and car enthusiast Giles Smith, and German engineer Bernard Friese, proved that a David could make its mark in a world of Goliaths, that what was essentially a tiny operation in not much more than a large shed could provide Wales with a company producing handbuilt GTs that it could truly be proud of.

However, the production of Gilbern cars was typical of small-scale British cars of the time in that, to avoid purchase tax, it could be sold unfinished. Gilberns were not exactly 'kit cars', but many finishing touches and final tweaks and specification were left to owners and dealers. Very few Gilberns are the same, as many tailored their cars for motorsport (the tough Gilbern made a good rally car), extra comfort or smoother running.

The first Gilberns were small sports cars based on MGs – first the Midget, secondly the B. However, in 1966 Smith and Friese decided to make a definite move on the low-volume British GT market with a car that, although it would be finished in typical tax-avoiding style, would have far more factory input and be redolent of the quality of, say, a Gordon-Keeble GK1.

The Genie was the first proper Gilbern GT car. Initially fitted with the smallest iteration of the Ford V6 – 2.5 litres – the Genie made light work of its fibreglass bodyshell, but the MGB-based components of the chassis meant that the car essentially strained on its leash. With the later option of the Capri GXL-specification 3-litre 'Essex' V6, the car could do 120mph, but suffered from serious chassis flex. The Genie was a promising start for Gilbern (selling 174 – more cars than all its previous output put together), but it was clear what needed improving.

One area definitely ahead of the game was the styling. Impressively for such a small company, the Gilbern Genie was sharply styled and reminiscent of the likes of the Gordon-Keeble GK1 and the Alfa Romeo Giulia GTV with its deep trapezoidal grille and sharp, swaged notchback shape. The basic shape stood it in good stead to last nearly ten years with only minor restyles.

The new Gilbern, called the 'Invader' (and aimed, therefore, at the sort of buyer that saw the Jensen Interceptor as aspirational), emerged in 1969. Although superficially it resembled a cleaned-up Genie (smooth bonnet, crisper edges, flush fittings), underneath it boasted vast improvements. A much stiffer, Ford-derived chassis coped much more ably with the V6 power – 141bhp – although the ride suffered somewhat; a Gilbern trademark was a slightly harder ride than many other GTs, signalling its sporting intent.

Broadening the Invader's appeal, on the other hand, were two overdrive ratios on the four-speed gearbox, and the option of a three-speed automatic. Stretching its versatility further was a vinyl-roofed sporting estate. Built only between 1971 and 1972, 105 customers opted for this capable and luxurious GT with space for one's belongings on a long trip.

Buoyed by its successes (366 Invader MkI, MkII and Estate models were made), Gilbern sought even greater sophistication with the Invader MkIII. A substantially restyled body, looking for all the world like an Alfa Romeo Giulia GTV with its traditional grille removed, and tough-looking extended wheelarches heralded the MkIII's 1972 arrival. Completely factory-built at Llantwit Major, the Invader III borrowed its suspension from the Ford Cortina/Taunus range making for a much smoother ride. The 144bhp V6 gave 125mph and 60mph in 7.2 seconds. The car was a consummate all-rounder at last, and today the most sought after version of the Invader – and, unfortunately, also the rarest Invader. 1973-74 brought the oil crisis, and the market for very low-volume, handbuilt GT cars dependent on components from larger companies dried up overnight. Only 195 Invader MkIIIs left Llantwit Major before the factory doors closed for good in late 1974.

SPECIFICATION
CYLINDERS = V6
CAPACITY (LITRES) = 2.5-3.0
POWER = 130-144BHP
TOP SPEED = 115-125MPH
TRANSMISSION = 4-SPEED MANUAL/3-SPEED AUTOMATIC
DESIGN = GILES SMITH & BERNARD FRIESE, GILBERN IN-HOUSE
BUILT = 1966-74

Motor *magazine tests the Gilbern Invader in the Welsh hills near the factory in October 1969. The handsome Genie and Invader series were more rugged than the average GT, and could handle road and rally stages with ease, as well as provide practical long-distance transport. (Courtesy David Hodges Collection)*

Gilbern may never have recovered but, of course, Ford did. As a result, the Genie and Invader might be exclusive and difficult to track down, but their running and maintenance certainly is not, and their ruggedness only helps the modern motoring situation. If you can find a Gilbern, and can appreciate its rugged quirks, it makes a dependable GT car. Invader MkII Estates and MkIII models are the most sought after, commanding upwards of £6000 today.

Jensen FF

It would be a mistake to consider the Jensen FF merely a variant of the Interceptor. True, it largely shared its body style with the Interceptor, and the 6.3-litre engine was identical to the Interceptor's first iteration, but there the similarities ended.

FF was an abbreviation of Ferguson Formula, the company renowned for its research into four-wheel drive systems on a variety of machinery, from experimental Formula 1 cars to tractors. Jensen, being a pioneering company (responsible for the first fibreglass four-seater, and for a time the builder of the fastest British GT too), perhaps sensed that the Interceptor was not radical enough to bear the name. Although it sold well, the Interceptor lacked the boldness of concept that makes a Jensen, and Ferguson offered a solution – a 4WD GT.

The 4WD system bestowed the big GT no greater power than its Interceptor sister, but what it did offer was a greater opportunity to use that power. Displacing 37 per cent of the Chrysler V8's power to the front wheels meant that the car suffered much less from the typical weight-induced understeer and snap oversteer (as a result of lack of grip) found in heavy GTs of the era. The powered front wheels allowed for sharp turn-in, and the power to the rear gave it a solid balance to counter the nose-heavy weight.

Outwardly, the only way to tell an FF from an Interceptor was the higher bonnet (disguised by slightly larger headlight surrounds and a taller grille), and two vents rather than one in the front wings to increase cooling for the brakes stopping the powered front wheels.

SPECIFICATION
CYLINDERS = V8
CAPACITY (LITRES) = 6.3
POWER = 330BHP
TOP SPEED = 130MPH
TRANSMISSION = 3-SPEED AUTOMATIC
DESIGN = ALFREDO VIGNALE, VIGNALE
BUILT = 1967-71
INNOVATION: THE FIRST FOUR-WHEEL DRIVE GT CAR

Of course, the infancy of four-wheel drive meant that there were fewer options on the FF than the Interceptor. The system was only calibrated to work with the 6.3-litre V8, for example (rather than the optional 7.2-litre in the Interceptor SP), and the only transmission accepted by the drivetrain was the three-speed Chrysler Torqueflite automatic – no manual was available.

Balancing these compromises were further new technologies. Another then-experimental system – Dunlop Maxaret anti-lock brakes (an early hydraulic system that oscillated the pressure on the brakes to simulate a fast cadence-brake and prevent locking) and all-round discs meant that not only would the FF corner more neatly than any other GT in its class, but also it would not slide so easily in an emergency situation if it were to lose traction. The all-round discs, rather than a mixture of discs and drums, helped further to eliminate the progressive brake fade that plagued many big GTs of the 1960s (in particular, the comparable Buick Riviera and Oldsmobile Toronado, both with drum brakes all round).

As such, not only was the FF solidly fast, it was one of the safest cars of its era, showcasing technology that would be seen as vital to road safety by the 1990s, and would not be properly attempted by another GT car until the Group B-era Audi Quattro of 1980.

The complexity of the FF – and its extra expense for no extra performance – turned most Jensen buyers' minds towards the Interceptor. For the 320 connoisseurs of automotive technology who bought the FF, however, they found their cars more useable, and safer on Alpine jaunts where changeable weather meant that many FFs arrived at their retreats with snow in the treads of their tires, yet ably, with much higher handling limits than any other GT. Nowadays, despite even greater thirst than the Interceptor (10mpg average), the qualities of the four-wheel drive, four-wheel disc, anti-lock brake FF still remain, although one must have a certain mechanical sympathy to use its potential properly. For such an advanced classic GT, the modern price is relatively low, and alternative fuel technology (such as LPG) can help reduce runnning costs.

There is a footnote to the FF story: in the world of 1970s Cold War espionage, the V8 grunt and pursuit stability of the Jensen FF led to its (bomb-proofed) floorplan being incorporated into Opel

The Ferguson Formula (FF) technology gave this Jensen superior traction on rough ground – ideal for the 'go anywhere' ethos of GT motoring. (Courtesy David Hodges Collection)

A Jensen FF was quite a different prospect compared to the Interceptor it bore a resemblance to. The extra vents in the front wings, and the taller bonnet and frontal aspect, give away the four-wheel drive hardware underneath. (Courtesy David Hodges Collection)

Senators issued to secret service operatives in West Germany. These were true undercover cars, featuring the latest tracking devices of the time, and a range of confusing headlight patterns hidden behind the grille for night pursuits. Perhaps, if 1960s spy thrillers had been more accurate, their lead characters would have driven Jensen FFs!

AC 428

Despite the lack of success with its previous GT, the Greyhound, AC decided to refine the infamous Cobra roadster into a proper GT car, mating the Greyhound's comforts with the Cobra's ferocious power and performance, and a bold touch of contemporary flash with the latest Italian styling.

Named according to the cubic inches of displacement in the Ford V8, the seven-litre 428 sported almost identical styling to the concurrent Maserati Mistral – a theme that recurred ten years later with the DeTomaso Longchamps and Maserati Kyalami. But that was of no matter – the Pietro Frua styling was truly classic. Marking the AC apart from the Maserati was a slightly larger front grille, bigger vents and more widely flared wheelarches, all in keeping with the car's more aggressive nature.

Yet it was a far calmer, more poised aggression than that of the Cobra. The sheer weight of the 428 over the lightweight Cobra roadster cut top speed by a hefty 20mph. The V8 was from the Ford Galaxie tin-top racer, bored out from 6998cc to 7014cc in the name of greater, smoother torque delivery (hence 428 instead of the famous '427' Cobra). It still managed 0-60mph in 6.2 seconds – absolutely ballistic for a 1960s GT car.

ITS ULTIMATE DEMEANOUR WAS ONE OF EXPLOSIVE SPEED AND TORQUE-BIASED CRUISING ABILITY.

The extra refinement was not just confined to the running gear, of course. The interior was a jet-setter's dream, with a wide, deeply-cowled instrument binnacle, all clad in leather, and the automatic transmission option featured a double-ended handle that looked like an aeroplane's throttle control, fronted by a bank of chunky switches. It screamed Learjet, and was a world apart from the basic flat panel found in the Cobra.

Effectively, the AC 428 belatedly replaced the Greyhound of the fifties. (Courtesy Roy Dowding)

Its ultimate demeanour was one of explosive speed and torque-biased cruising ability. The 428 featured softer, friendlier suspension too, and American power-assisted steering from Ford which, although it made the car easy to pilot, detracted somewhat from the sporting nature. However, this was a GT while the Cobra was the raw, unassisted beast.

The appeal of the 428 was expanded two years after its launch, in 1968, with a convertible version. The added wind in the hair and scuttle-shake of the convertible took the 428 concept closer to the Cobra. It was remarkably successful (for a small-scale AC GT car), and due to its lack of a roof, and thus lighter weight, had a higher straight-line top speed (close to 145mph).

Unfortunately for AC, it suffered the curse of AC GTs – lack of demand. The Cobra truly cemented AC's reputation as the builder of the world's ultimate sports cars, not leather-lined GTs, no matter how accomplished they were. Also, the 428 did struggle for its own identity alongside the already-established and recognisable Maserati Mistral – it did not sport the traditional AC grille or curved tail. As a result, only 81 AC 428s were built, a large proportion (29) being convertibles.

Their reliability, due to the unstressed, cruising Galaxie V8, and proven systems and drivetrain, is of no worry – not even for today's owner – although the thirst of the V8 and the potential for the body corrosion should not be underestimated. However, with so few examples built, AC clubs will have kept tabs on them. Their prices are a reflection of the care and restoration afforded to them by their owners. They are rarely for sale, but as the 'civilized Cobra', they are highly sought after GTs for owners who appreciate high power as well as luxury.

SPECIFICATION
CYLINDERS = V8
CAPACITY (LITRES) = 7.0
POWER = 345BHP
TOP SPEED = 142-144MPH
TRANSMISSION = 4-SPEED MANUAL/3-SPEED AUTOMATIC
DESIGN = PIETRO FRUA, FRUA
BUILT = 1966-72

AC is said to have requested Frua to design a Maserati Mistral lookalike. The similarities cannot be ignored.
(Courtesy Martin Brewer)

Interiors were strongly influenced by the flightdeck idioms of the sixties jet set. Note the 'throttle'-shaped automatic gear lever.
(Courtesy Martin Brewer)

Lotus Elan +2

The Lotus Elan was one of the greatest sports cars of the 1960s, boasting handling neater than any other comparable car, and a lightweight fibreglass body that allowed the small Lotus twin-cam engine to propel the car with a rate of acceleration (6.6 seconds to 60mph on the fastest model) that rivalled the likes of the Jaguar E-type on the track. The refinement of the X-shaped steel backbone chassis was unrivalled, and the ride comfort, far from being off-putting, hard and jarring, was smooth and unruffled. Like Lotus' previous sporting effort, the Elite, it managed overwhelming sophistication in terms of suspension technology, but unlike the unsoundproofed, fixed-window, fibreglass-monocoque Elite, a long journey was not just the preserve of the racing driver or the masochist.

It held many of the qualities to be a great GT car. In fact, Toyota built its beautiful 2000GT sports car on the chassis of an Elan, but its dimensions made it so cramped that, when Eon producers wanted Sean Connery to travel in one for 1967's *You Only Live Twice*, a one-off convertible had to be made. The standard Elan was also cramped inside, lacked many luxuries, and could be built as a kit to avoid purchase tax.

However, in 1967, purchase tax was close to being revoked, the mainstream motoring scene greatly respected the abilities of Lotus cars, and the market was ripe for a different kind of GT car. Enter the Lotus Elan +2.

The +2 shared the standard Elan backbone chassis, suspension and running gear, and thus its exemplary handling, but what set it apart was a larger body, maximising the space inside for a pair of smaller occupants in the rear. Rather than being merely a variant of the Elan, the +2 was a separate car in its own right. Styled by Ron Hickman (who designed the small Elan sports car too), the lines of the +2 were flowing, cohesive, and modern, with a smooth waistline, low air intake and pop-up headlights. Knock-off steel wheels gave the car the demeanour of a small Ferrari 330 GTC, even though its nearest rival, in terms of engine size, abilities and cost, was the Alfa Romeo Giulia GTV.

The Elan +2 was also relatively luxuriously trimmed compared to the Elan sports car: leather seats were an option, and a walnut dashboard, electric windows, cigarette lighter and multiple-speed windscreen wipers became available in 1968,

when the whole Lotus range was refreshed, largely due to Gold Leaf sponsorship on the Team Lotus Formula 1 cars, when the Seven S3 and Elan S4 also benefited.

SPECIFICATION
CYLINDERS = 4
CAPACITY (LITRES) = 1.6
POWER = 115-130BHP
TOP SPEED = 118-121MPH
TRANSMISSION = 4/5-SPEED MANUAL
DESIGN = RON HICKMAN, LOTUS IN-HOUSE
BUILT = 1967-74

The car dropped the 'Elan' tag and became a separate model with its own identity, the 'Plus 2S'. VAT replaced Purchase Tax in 1968 too, and the advantages of providing kit cars rather than full production models disappeared.

But the most important aspect of the Plus 2 series is that it presaged a new type of GT car that would succeed in the post-oil crisis future when so many other hopefuls would fail. Rather than resorting to the widely-available power of big, cheap American V8s, hefty chassis, large proportions and steel bodies, the Plus 2 embraced the Lotus philosophy in a capable GT – a high-revving, refined Ford-based powerplant, a proven, sporting chassis, compact dimensions and lightweight, aerodynamic fibreglass cladding. It pointed to a future of greater efficiency and less decadence, where greatness would not just be measured in size and extravagance in every way, but carefully metered modernism and engineering. Whilst Lotus would continue with the theme, it is evident that the efficiency of the Plus 2 kept Lotus afloat during the fuel crisis years when so many others failed.

One thing that the Plus 2 unfortunately could not escape was questionable Lotus build quality. The modifications made to the Ford engine to create the Lotus twin-cam unit often resulted in overheating, and the electrical systems were notoriously unreliable.

The Lotus Elan +2, only available in fully-built form, was the first sign that Lotus intended to challenge the Italian big guns. Some find this shape more elegant than the 2-seater Elan sports car, and the interior was definitely a luxurious place to be compared to Lotus' previous coupé, the Elite. (Courtesy David Hodges Collection)

Things were improved with the Plus 2S 130 of 1971. The engine, termed 'Big Valve' on account of its larger valves and more bespoke cooling systems, made for 130bhp (hence the name). This made for 120mph top speed, and acceleration to 60mph in 7.4 seconds, putting it in the class of the Jaguar XKE 2+2 of the same era, but with essentially less than half the displacement, and two fewer cylinders, such was the efficiency and economy of its design. The Big Valve was fitted to all Lotus cars – Elan Sprint, Europa Special, Plus 2S 130 and Seven SS – of the era.

The final flowering of the Plus 2S was the 130/5 of 1972-74. The '/5' referred to the 5-speed gearbox appropriated by Lotus from the Austin Maxi and heavily modified. Although it suffered from some reliability issues, when it was 'on song' it allowed the driver to make the most of the 'Big Valve' engine's range,

edging the top speed past 120mph. Even so, Lotus realised the compromises of the small Plus 2S, and it gave way to the bigger, more modern Elite 500 in late 1974.

The Plus 2 will be remembered as the first compact GT car, one that seemed so modern alongside the thirsty dinosaurs that would be rendered anachronistic in 1973-74. Today, specialists such as Spyder have tackled its deficiencies, fitting galvanised chassis, modern electrics, and even modern Ford Zetec engines on throttle bodies, plus Ford transmissions and braking systems, making the car a reliable long-distance GT for the modern era, as well as a tough and capable sports car. Others, such as Christopher Neil, have made it a convincing convertible. Its relatively low price, frugal engine and potential for greater practicality makes it not only one of the best cars of the 1960s, but of the modern era, too.

Ferrari 365GT 2+2 & GTC/4

With the 365GT 2+2, the truly luxurious Ferraris hit the mainstream markets. Whereas previously the majority of Ferraris had been stradale racing thinking with concessions to GT comfort, and small numbers of exclusive, order-only luxury supercars aimed at the US market usually tagged Superfast, Superamerica and California, the 365GT 2+2 marked the point where the Ferrari road and race car programmes became well and truly separated. While the Scuderia still contributed to the engine and gearbox technology, the rest of the car was pure, comfortable 1960s Grand Tourer.

Major mechanical concessions to luxury included a heavily insulated prop shaft to reduce noise and vibration in the well-appointed cabin. Road-focused Michelin tyres replaced the traditional race-bred Ferrari-sanctioned Firestones. As well as air conditioning, the car boasted such quirks as small electric motors attached to the hinges on the opening quarterlights to keep them shut if they detected rattling at high speeds.

In style, it resembled a truncated version of the traditional Ferrari form, with cowled headlights, oval grille and flat tail, with interesting integration of signalling lights into the chromework. However, one thing that could not be avoided were the massive dimensions; inspired by the 365 California Spider special, it had more in common with a big American GT than a smaller, traditional European one. However, America was the 365GT 2+2's largest market; this is what a driver of a Buick Riviera moved up to, rather than the driver of a Ferrari 330GTC.

This deviance from the accepted Ferrari norm predictably drew criticism. Some road testers politely suggested that it was more like an Aston Martin than a Ferrari, more British or American in its heavy, road-crushing nature than an Italian car, yet the power steering and sheer weight of 4025lb certainly diluted the traditional Ferrari savagery.

The greatest saving grace was, of course, the V12 engine. Developed from Le Mans racing practise with mid-engined racers, the 365 expansion to 4.4 litres offered traditional Ferrari revs with massive torque.

It was clear that there were areas for improvement in the 365GT 2+2 – compared to other Ferraris of the era it wasn't

The 365GT 2+2 was clearly inspired by Ferrari's racing cars, but was much bigger and heavier, geared towards the American market. (Courtesy Justin Banks)

SPECIFICATION
CYLINDERS = V12
CAPACITY (LITRES) = 4.4
POWER = 320-340BHP
TOP SPEED = 151-152MPH
TRANSMISSION = 5-SPEED MANUAL
DESIGN = SERGIO PININFARINA/LEONARDO FIORAVANTI, PININFARINA
BUILT = 1967-72

These lines are undeniably graceful. Few 365GT 2+2s were specified in traditional rosso corsa, the subtler hues suiting less ostentatious owners. (Courtesy Justin Banks)

From the rear, the massive overhang becomes evident. The gait of the 365GT 2+2 was more akin to an Aston Martin than, say, a 330GTC. (Courtesy Justin Banks)

much of a driver's car. However, salvation for the Ferrari über-GT arrived with a new era of Ferraris in general, heralded by the 365GTB/4 'Daytona'. The new supercar reinvigorated Ferrari – combining the ultimate development of the 365 V12, new wedge-shaped styling, and Lotus-style weight-saving measures such as fibreglass floorplan and engine bulkheads, plus an improved drag coefficient.

The thinking behind the Daytona was then applied to the idea of the big Ferrari GT. The new 1971 365GTC/4 drew strongly on the Daytona's styling, with a narrow front grille, a big swooping wedge profile, a bold bank of six tail-lights at the rear, and a blade-like rear window profile adding individuality. Pop-up headlights and great gashed vents on the bonnet were pure Daytona. Four-cam Daytona technology upped the power of the V12 to 340 brake horsepower. Although this offered no

The Ferrari's sumptuous interior was one of the last of the breed to use wood veneer and a leather-clad gear lever. Later interiors used a greater amount of weight-saving trim. (Courtesy Justin Banks)

The wedge-like Ferrari 365GTC/4 was the Daytona supercar's civilised, grand touring cousin, and represents something of a bargain Daytona alternative these days. The rear end, with its upward-slashing window line, influenced the Rover SD1 and the Aston Martin Ogle DBSS. (Courtesy David Hodges Collection)

greater top speed (this was still a very heavy car), the 0-60mph dash was cut dramatically from 7.1 seconds, to 6.3.

The 365GTC/4 marked the arrival of a new era, an era where the word 'supercar', rather than 'GT', marked out the ultimate road car experience. The C/4 no longer sat at the top of the Ferrari tree, but below the Daytona, representative of a truly savage breed of cars where comfort and usability was sacrificed for ultimate speed.

Unfortunately, the 365GTC/4 only lasted two years before it fell foul of incoming safety regulations. Criticisms were also levelled at the finish of the cockpit, which used such materials as plastic and tweed in an attempt at early 1970s modernism that angered the tifosi. It was replaced by the 365GT4 in late 1972, which stepped even further away from the traditional Ferrari

recipe than the 365GT 2+2 had done, but by 1973, the entire car market had changed forever.

Today, the market treats the 365GT 2+2 and 365GTC/4 very differently. The 2+2 has been largely forgotten, and its attributes are still not favourably remembered by Ferrari aficionados. However, to appreciators of the GT form, it is a suave V12 express with thoroughbred underpinnings at a bargain price relative to other Ferraris of the era.

The C/4, on the other hand, is appreciated as a cut-price Daytona. It features most of the styling, engine and presence that made the Daytona great, but at a much lower price, and with comparable exclusivity considering its short production run.

Both, in their own ways, are great GTs.

Mercedes-Benz CE/SE

Visually based on the 220/250 saloon of 1967 and powered by the 2.8-litre engine found in the SL roadster, the first Mercedes-Benz Grand Tourer since the pre-war Art Deco beauties of the 1930s was the 250CE. Retaining the saloon's engine designation for a sense of identity, this pillarless two-door coupé represented the German firm's re-emergence as a true luxury contender in the 1960s. Sports cars and coachbuilt limousines aside, Mercedes-Benz had survived post-war largely by building rather staid, conservative saloons such as the 190 'Ponton', mainly for the home market, and rugged utility cars for taxi and desert use. Mercedes' image had been relying on the halo effect cast by its glamorous SL series since the 1950s; these new Grand Tourers returned luxury, long-distance travel to the middle of the range, and aimed it squarely at all markets, from the autobahns of Germany to the highways of America.

A rather conservative design for Paul Bracq (who, in contrast, is most famous for the BMW M1's outlandish and modernist Turbo concept forerunner), it made a proper coupé design out of the previous 2-door reduction of the saloon, the 220/300. The design, whilst predictable in the eyes of European fans of the marque, was to be highly influential in the USA. The arrival of the Mercedes-Benz on American shores led to the following generation of Cadillacs, Lincolns and Chryslers sporting stacked headlights, trimmed fins and square chrome grilles, all in an attempt to emulate European sophistication. The sparsely chromed wraparound glass would become a Mercedes trademark, and the distinctive rear glass semi-fastback would be seen on the car's successors right up to the twenty-first century.

After predictable success, Mercedes-Benz decided to make the Grand Tourer a model in its own right, the 280CE accurately mirroring the size of the engine. Despite being much heavier than the 280SL sports car, it was no wallowing barge, propelling the car to a top speed of 125mph, with the typical Mercedes air suspension ride – firm compared to American cars, pliant compared to European ones – satisfying on either side of the Atlantic. All-round disc brakes meant it stopped far short of comparable American cars too.

It was joined in 1969 by the 280SE, the letter change signalling the influence of the new Mercedes-Benz S-Class dynasty, which would go on to be regarded by some as the best luxury saloon car in the world in all its guises. The SE was coachbuilt alongside the 600 Limousine, rather than on the production line with lesser CE models. As well as the greater levels of luxury, an SE could be spotted by its four, round, unglazed headlights, dictated by new American safety regulations.

The biggest difference, however, was under the bonnet. Despite its 280 nomenclature, the SE featured a 3.5-litre V8 engine. Although top speed only rose marginally over the CE's (128mph as opposed to 125), it was the autobahn-storming acceleration that impressed most. With 60mph coming up in under ten seconds, the 280SE 3.5 was remarkably quick for a big, heavy, (usually) automatic GT of the 1960s.

Today, the market for these big Mercedes is divided. The 280SE 3.5-litre coupé, and especially the virtually depreciation-proof convertible, command large price tags due to their meticulous coachbuilt nature and more glamorous, unstressed power units, so expect to pay between £24,000 and £45,000. Alongside these, the 220, 250 and 280SE are underrated bargains, with all the looks and abilities of the big V8 cars, but without the price tag. They are less likely to have survived as well though, and are not immune to heavy rust, although the longevity and reliability of all Mercedes engines is legendary. These cars remain among the world's great GT cruisers.

SPECIFICATION
CYLINDERS = 6/V8
CAPACITY (LITRES) = 2.2-3.5
POWER = 170-200BHP
TOP SPEED = 125-127MPH
TRANSMISSION = 5-SPEED MANUAL/4-SPEED AUTOMATIC
DESIGN = PAUL BRACQ, IN-HOUSE MERCEDES-BENZ
BUILT = 1968-76

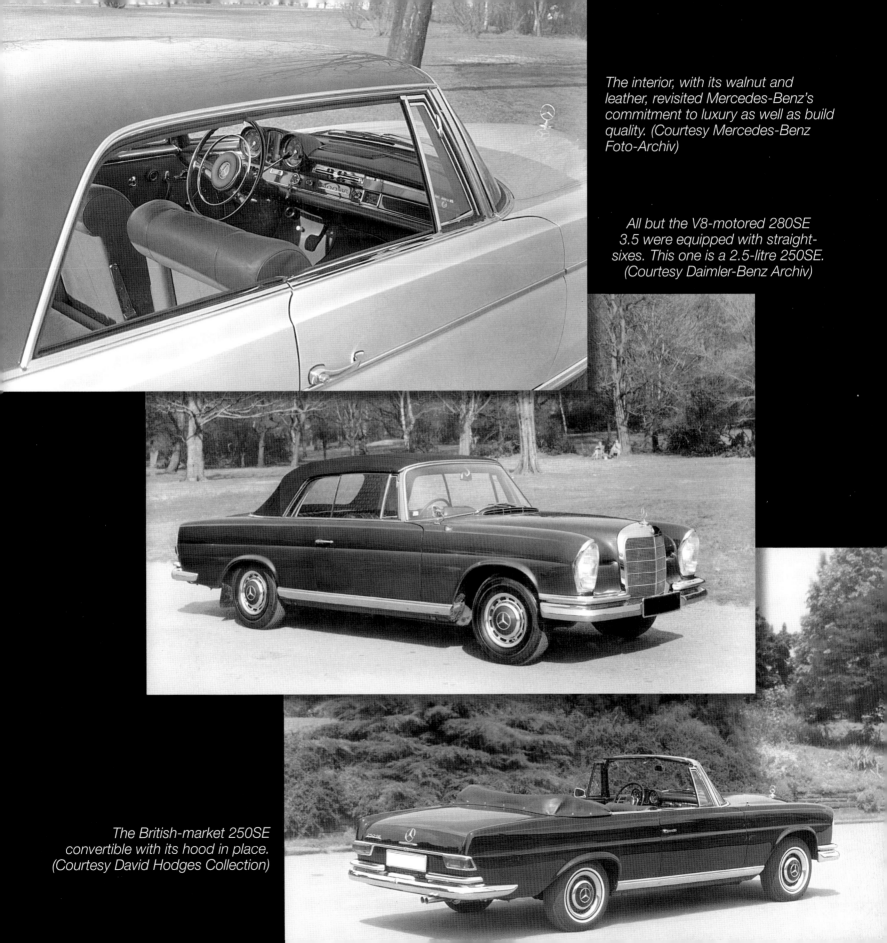

The interior, with its walnut and leather, revisited Mercedes-Benz's commitment to luxury as well as build quality. (Courtesy Mercedes-Benz Foto-Archiv)

All but the V8-motored 280SE 3.5 were equipped with straight-sixes. This one is a 2.5-litre 250SE. (Courtesy Daimler-Benz Archiv)

The British-market 250SE convertible with its hood in place. (Courtesy David Hodges Collection)

Lamborghini Espada & Jarama

Few other GTs are as representative of the jet set as the Lamborghini Espada. Emerging into the world the same year as Concorde, the Espada elevated the GT concept to new heights, as a GT car specifically designed with four fully

SPECIFICATION
CYLINDERS = V12
CAPACITY (LITRES) = 4.0
POWER = 325-365BHP
TOP SPEED = 154-162MPH
TRANSMISSION = 5-SPEED MANUAL/3-SPEED AUTOMATIC
DESIGN = MARCELLO GANDINI, BERTONE
BUILT = 1968-78

appointed seats, rather than a compromised two-plus-two, retaining all the power and outrageousness associated with the marque that brought the world the Miura.

The Espada driver sat behind a four-litre V12 and an impressive bank of instruments that would not have looked out of place in Concorde either. Unlike Ferrari, Lamborghini obliged its customers' desires with bold and striking colour schemes. The Espada driver wanted for nothing – air conditioning, power steering, an 8-track stereo, electric windows and electrically adjustable seats completed the picture of ultimate comfort, and ultimate power – 325bhp from the first Espada V12.

It could have been even more extreme and futuristic: The Marzal show car that preceded the production Espada featured a rear-mounted transverse slant-six (half a Miura block), a shin-high front end, a menacing bank of six headlights, an interior upholstered in silver leather, and most dramatically, huge glass gullwing doors that ran the length of the bodywork. It appeared as a guest pace car in the Monaco Grand Prix of 1966, driven by Monte Carlo royalty.

Reality brought the concept back from outer space, but only as far as the stratosphere. Picking up on the high visibility afforded by the Marzal, the Espada featured huge glass areas – a panoramic windscreen, a long, almost horizontal glass hatch (a styling feature picked up by Larry Shinoda on his design for the 1971-73 iteration of the Ford Mustang

The striking Gandini-styled Espada took grand touring themes to the extreme, with a long, wide, exaggerated 'international' look. The one-piece glass gullwing doors of the Marzal concept car were dropped, however.
(Courtesy David Hodges Collection)

A glimpse of super-luxury, 1968-style. Note the radio in front of the passenger, and an aftermarket cassette player, dictation machine, telephone and loudspeaker on the driver's side (with the cable doubtlessly set to interfere with their knees!). (Courtesy David Hodges Collection)

Another ingenious aspect to the Espada's design was its use of glass. The massive, upswept rear windows, glass one-piece hatch and glazed rear panel aids visibility when driving this huge car. (Courtesy David Hodges Collection)

The thoroughbred 4-litre V12 that powered all Lamborghinis from the 400GT to the Countach LP400. Enlarged versions still power today's Lamborghinis. (Courtesy David Hodges Collection)

fastback), a glass panel above the rear lights to aid reversing, and a low waistline combined with a high roof, making for a huge glasshouse with massive, sharp-edged windows. For a car over ten feet long and six feet wide, the contribution of the glass to manoeuvring was invaluable.

The car instantly sold well, appealing to buyers with the necessary financial means, who loved the outrageousness of Lamborghini but wanted four-seat practicality and greater comfort and space than afforded by the Miura supercar.

Alongside the second series of the Espada, released in 1970, a smaller two-plus-two Lamborghini, called the Jarama, emerged into the range. Featuring the new 350bhp V12, the Jarama was intended as an 'entry level' Lamborghini. It sported chunkier bodywork similar to the contemporary Iso Lele, but retained the aggressive four-headlight squint and severe NACA ducting seen on its bigger Espada brother.

As well as being smaller and cheaper, the Jarama was a more sporting drive. Being lighter and more compact meant that the V12 produced performance closer to the Miura. The Jarama was more conventional too, with a bootlid as opposed to a hatch, and more restricted rear legroom than the Espada. Still, it did not sell as well as the more radical Espada – Lamborghini was increasingly being associated with bold and aggressive modernism rather than conventionality, and although it was an excellent car – Lamborghini's most sporting four-seater – it faded into the background.

More power from the V12 (365bhp) in 1973 made its way into the Espada Series 3 and the Jarama 'S' (the standard 350bhp Jarama was retained as a base model, but still the Espada outsold it); by now though, even the Espada's sales were dropping off in favour of the increasingly outlandish Countach. The Espada and Jarama continued unchanged until 1978, when they were dropped. Lamborghini had already been concentrating on its more fuel crisis-friendly Urraco range. Now, however, the marque is looking into a 'new' Espada, over twenty-five years after the original's demise.

Today, the long-lived Espada is the cheapest way into V12 Lamborghini ownership, as they have depreciated massively

The rationalisation continued inside, although mounting the switchgear on a 'tray' in front of the driver was unique. (Courtesy David Hodges Collection)

(though their running costs are possibly even greater than those of the Miura and Countach), and so represent temptingly accessible glamour. The Jarama, however, is ironically now a more expensive and exclusive car than the model it was only intended to supplement. It is also a more sporting and manageable car, although the costs incurred by the V12 should never be underestimated.

Still, if any single car represents the pinnacle of the Age d'Or of the GT car, the otherworldly Espada is most definitely it.

The Jarama was intended to be a toned-down, less controversial alternative to the Espada, and was marketed as an (expensive) entry level model. This approach was to prove unfruitful. (Courtesy David Hodges Collection)

Reliant Scimitar GTE & GTC

Very rarely does an individually-commissioned design variation on an existing car go on to dominate the rest of the range, but, in 1968, the specially-bodied shooting-brake estate version of HRH Prince Phillip's Reliant Scimitar, 'productionised' in a new design by Ogle's Tom Karen, replaced the standard Scimitar GT Series 4 in Reliant's sporting range. It was at this point that Reliant's image would take a dramatic turn for the better for the best part of two decades.

Far from being related to questionable quality finishes and associations with three-wheeled microcars, Tom Karen styled the GTE (Grand Touring Estate) as a GT car capable of not only fulfilling the luxury continent-crossing role, but also capable of being used as a practical everyday car; it could accommodate large loads of luggage, was spacious enough for four passengers, and was adaptable too – the rear seats could be folded flat in a variety of combinations depending on the rear load. The Scimitar GTE was a sporting GT car you could take on holiday without compromising on the amount of luggage.

Tom Karen's styling instantly recalled the Jensen Interceptor and exclusively converted Aston Martin shooting-brakes. As for the most part, the frontal styling was a 'Series 5' upgrade of the already-handsome Scimitar, although Karen made the nose sharper, with squarer light surrounds and an overhung grille like bared shark's teeth. The rest of the bodywork, however, was strikingly radical. Large rear windows angled upwards, away from a smoothly descending waistline towards the tail of the car, whilst a crisp, moulded swage line ran between the two. The design ended in a purposeful-looking opening glass rear window, suspended on extending struts, that somehow managed to avoid the traditional estate car image of looking resolutely unsporting. It is interesting how many modern estate-builders with sporting intent, such as Alfa Romeo and Volvo, have copied the 1968 Reliant's tough lines and semi-fastback shape to avoid a stale, unsporting appearance.

Performance was in keeping with a proper GT too. With a 135bhp Ford 'Essex' 3-litre V6 and lightweight fibreglass body, even the slowest automatic iteration of the car did 120mph. With the manual overdrive gearbox, 125mph and 60mph coming up in a little over ten seconds made the GTE an enticing prospect

SPECIFICATION
CYLINDERS = V6
CAPACITY (LITRES) = 3.0-2.9
POWER = 135-150BHP
TOP SPEED = 118-130MPH
TRANSMISSION = 4-SPEED MANUAL/3-SPEED AUTOMATIC
DESIGN = TOM KAREN, OGLE DESIGN
BUILT = 1968-90
INNOVATION: BROUGHT ESTATE PRACTICALITY TO THE VOLUME GT MARKET

A Scimitar GTE on tour. Forty years on, its combination of rust-free bodywork, simplicity, practicality and reliability make it an extremely appealing prospect. (Courtesy David Poole)

The Scimitar GTE proved an unprecedented success with the country house set. HRH Prince Philip owned the first example, and HRH Princess Anne has had countless examples – she currently owns a Middlebridge Scimitar.
(Courtesy David Hodges Collection)

for drivers looking to reconcile their passion for fast cars with a need for practicality.

And it sold strongly too. The only comparable opposition for the car at the time was the Gilbern Invader MkII Estate, a low-key, low-production affair which, despite sharing almost every specification with the Reliant (Ford V6, fibreglass body, same gearboxes, practical layout), could not compete with Reliant's accomplished marketing programme. "When you own a Scimitar GTE, you'll have a lot of explaining to do", ran Reliant's advertising lines.

As it began as a Royal commissioned car, the GTE did not

take long to find favour with Buckingham Palace once again when, in 1970, HRH Princess Anne acquired her first of a dynasty of eight. For Reliant, a company which still made the Robin, Regal and Rialto three-wheelers, this image boost was nothing short of incredible.

In reaction, the car was updated in 1975 to 'Series 6A' specification. In order to distance the car with Reliant's economy output, 'Scimitar' became a marque in its own right, and the distinctive sword badge would still be seen on another range of small sports cars well into the 1990s. The Scimitar GTE Series 6A retained the mechanical specifications of its predecessor, but the new body style suggested greater weight and solidity, with chunkier fittings, flared wheelarches, fatter Wolfrace alloys and a bluff nose almost identical to the Interceptor, wearing a strip of chrome with 'Scimitar' printed upon it. The interior practicality was complimented with greater luxury – bigger seats and all the options the Ford parts bin could afford made the GTE a genuine luxury coupé contender in the louche late-1970s.

However, the car was also made heavier, blunting performance. Only 118mph was available from the ageing Essex V6, and although the car still sold well, Reliant was anxious for a new engine to bring the GTE back to expectations.

Salvation came in 1980 in the form of Ford's new 2.8-litre 'Cologne' V6. Fuel-injected and putting out 150bhp, it brought performance back up to the levels of the first, slimmer GTE. A greater tendency to rev made for a 0-60mph time of 8.9 seconds.

Alongside this new engine (in the 'Series 6B' GTE), came a new convertible variant, the GTC. Long-awaited, and doing away with the estate practicality of the GTE, the GTC boasted an ingenious roof that featured a 'laudalette'-style fold-down canvas section over the rear passengers, and a rigid 'targa' roof over the front, meaning coupé-style practicality and safety when needed, but with the possibility of open-top motoring when the weather suited. It was a system largely copied from the 1971 Triumph Stag, but it was an effective way of engineering a GT convertible without the need for a bulky, difficult-to-accommodate hardtop, and the Stag was three years dead when the GTC arrived on the scene.

In the end, the Scimitar GTE was a victim of its own success as cheaper cars that offered the same, such as the Volvo 480ES, and the rise of the 'hot hatch' forced Grand Tourers – even eminently practical ones – further from view. By 1986, a hatchback was nothing special and the Scimitar appeared rather old and

With its folding seats, the rear section of a GTE has more luggage space than the average supermini. If you were looking for a value-for-money 'car for life', the Scimitar might just be it. (Courtesy David Poole)

tired. The role of Scimitar convertible passed from the GTC to the SS1 sports car, and Reliant discontinued the GTE.

However, that was not the end to the story. A company named Middlebridge bought the GTE design and updated it thoroughly, replacing outdated chrome with lightweight plastic, making the interior even more luxurious, and fitting the biggest 2.9-litre fuel-injected V6 from the then-new Ford Granada Scorpio. 130mph was possible from the Middlebridge GTE. Princess Anne was, predictably, a Middlebridge customer, and still owns her GTE.

For today's owner, these cars offer everything they did a prospective buyer back in 1968 – a rust-free body, reliable, manageable engine and much practicality. Their ubiquity on the English classic car

Early and late GTEs compared. The car on the right is a Series 5, introduced in 1968. The car on the left is a Series 6, available from 1975 to 1991. By 1975, 'Scimitar' was a separate brand operated by Reliant. (Courtesy David Poole)

scene (over 15,000 were built) makes them perhaps less exclusive than the Jensens and Aston Martins they emulated, but for the thrill of owning a 1960s-style GT car, with all the qualities expected of it, their low price is thoroughly welcome. The higher prices are reserved for GTCs and Middlebridge GTEs, but examples of the other models are plentiful, reliable, and cheap.

Aston Martin DBS V8, DBSS, V8, Vantage, Volante & Zagato

The William Towns-designed Aston Martin DBS really was a great car in search of a greater engine. In fact, it had been designed around a 4.8-litre V8 unit first proposed by Aston Martin's engine genius Tadek Marek back in 1965, but problems with the bottom-end forced the perfectionist Marek back to the drawing board while the DBS, fitted with Marek's earlier 4-litre straight-six, emerged as the successor to the DB6, marking the end of an Aston Martin era. Still, the wide dimensions of the DBS promised a more powerful future for Towns' Detroit muscle-influenced design.

In 1969, the new quad-cam, 5.3-litre V8 was ready. Producing a creditable 325bhp (far below its potential but the unit was not yet completely proven), it was installed in a revamped DBS, titled 'DBS V8'. The DBS V8 had lower front and rear valances to accommodate the heftier running gear, the bigger engine and

its cannon-like exhaust pipes, and was fitted with massive, road-crushing magnesium alloy wheels in place of the DBS' dainty wires.

The car met with general approval, although some dared to decry it as merely an expensive muscle car, and not particularly powerful in that American-led field either. The truth is, it was a GT in the best Aston Martin traditions, and was never intended as anything else. Everything about it was respectable – the trim styling, the power output, the traction-based handling, and the tasteful interior. To cement the GT image, one was driven by Roger Moore in *The Persuaders* TV series (though the car in question belonged to circus impresario Billy Smart, and was in fact a six-cylinder car fitted with V8 badges and dubbed with a V8 soundtrack).

Before Aston Martin improved on the design, Tom Karen of

SPECIFICATION
CYLINDERS = V8
CAPACITY (LITRES) = 5.3
POWER = 325-432BHP
TOP SPEED = 160-190MPH
TRANSMISSION = 5-SPEED MANUAL/3-SPEED AUTOMATIC
DESIGN = WILLIAM TOWNS, ASTON MARTIN/TOM KAREN, OGLE/ERCOLE SPADA, ZAGATO
BUILT = 1969-90

The Aston Martin V8 was first installed in the William Towns-designed DBS, which dated back to 1967. (Courtesy David Hodges Collection)

This restyle, with single headlights each side of the grille, was applied in 1973 to both the V8 and six-cylinder Aston Martins, although the 'six' only lasted another year. (Courtesy David Hodges Collection)

Ogle developed a special-bodied three-seater version called the DBSS. Commissioned by Sotheby Cigarettes as a promotional vehicle, the DB Sotheby Special was an instant hit at motorshows in 1971, featuring a wedge-shaped profile similar to a Ferrari 365 GTC/4, reflective Triplex glass (an Ogle trademark), and two banks of eleven tail-lights, designed to show how intensely the car was braking and how severely it was turning. It is interesting to note that today's engineers are using LED lights to a similar end. Three examples of the DBSS were made, one in gold-pinstriped maroon, one in navy blue and one in Aston Martin 'Storm Red'. The red one is now endowed with a 7-litre engine conversion. The navy blue example was painted white for another promotion but later written off in a crash.

Perhaps spurred on by Ogle's progressive take on the V8, William Towns penned the official update in 1972. Aston Martin, suffering financial crisis, emerged triumphant with the new car, simply called the V8. Although the six-cylinder model was retained until 1974 as an entry-level car (named AM Vantage), it was clear that this design was to be the new face of Aston Martin. One deep-set headlight at each side, and a stepped air intake even more suggestive of Detroit than the DBS full-width modernist take on the Aston Martin trademark signalled the greater muscle – 340bhp of it – within. It was a beautiful car, yet financial problems plagued Aston Martin, and, in 1972, David Brown sold the company to Company Developments, an asset-stripper, and his name disappeared from the famous winged badge. One year before the impending oil crisis, Aston Martin spiralled towards receivership.

Carroll Shelby, of Cobra fame, offered to buy the company and continue where AC's cars had left off with Ford V8s, but Aston Martin resisted this attack on its thoroughbred nature. Then came the oil crisis, and it would seem the death knell had been sounded for thirsty cars like Aston Martins. By 1974, the Newport Pagnell factory had ceased production.

William Towns freely admitted to being influenced by Detroit muscle cars, especially with the rear styling. This is the 1977 170mph Vantage version, instantly recognisable by its blanked-off grille, air dam and rear spoiler
(Courtesy David Hodges Collection)

Inevitably, there was a convertible version, the V8 Volante. Some people believe this version, without the American-style roofline, is more elegant. (Courtesy David Hodges Collection)

Miraculously, the company survived where so many other big name, small-volume GT makers – Jensen, Iso and so on – had floundered. The marque had many rich aficionados, who donated money in charitable gestures to keep the company alive.

The price of a V8 went up dramatically, from £7000 to £9000 (bear in mind that a new Ferrari Daytona cost £10,000), and it marked a sea change in the GT market – higher oil prices meant that car choice was not only based on what a customer could afford to buy, but also to run. Whilst many other companies pulled out altogether, or downsized to four- or six-cylinder engines, Aston Martin joined a new, stratospheric elite of cars for persons for whom high petrol prices were a minor inconvenience. Only Jaguar and Mercedes-Benz bridged this rift in the market.

This launched the Aston Martin V8 into a new era of success. As well as supplementing a new range of four-door Lagonda versions of the V8, as many luxuries as could be managed found their way onto the V8 – electric central locking, more wood and leather, and cruise control joined a new rear end style incorporating a flat-tailed spoiler on the series 4 'Oscar India' (ie, OI – 'October Introduction') of 1978.

Accompanying the Oscar India were two supplementary models, the Volante convertible version, and the now-legendary Vantage. With its engine based on Aston Martin's Nimrod racing car, the V8 Vantage, with 380bhp (later 400), signalled by a blanked-off, body-coloured radiator grille and a deep front spoiler raced, ballistic, into the record books as the fastest-accelerating production car of the time – 0-60mph in 5.4 seconds, with a maximum of 170mph. The success – and exorbitant price – of the Aston Martin continued into the 1980s (by which point nearly everyone involved in the music business from Duran Duran to Judas Priest seem to have owned one at some time or other), when extravagance dictated a Vantage Volante (a convertible Vantage) be constructed. Aston Martin was initially uncomfortable with the idea, worried that the hood could detach itself at high speeds, but the Vantage Volante – bespoiled, colour-coded, and wearing huge wheelarches and side-skirts – emerged in 1986, and one was driven by Timothy Dalton in the following year's James Bond adventure, *The Living Daylights*. It marked the last of the traditional V8 shape, by then twenty years old, and past its best aesthetically. HRH Prince Charles, a serial Aston Martin customer, ordered a Vantage Volante especially lacking in aerodynamic add-ons, and the 'PoW' (Prince of Wales) specification became an expensive factory option for the discerningly wealthy.

But the V8 itself was nowhere near past its best. Also in 1986, Zagato in Italy set about producing a special flush-glazed, lightweight version of the V8. Looking severe and controversial in traditional Zagato fashion, the angular V8 Vantage Zagato pumped out 432bhp, enabling nearly 190mph, all without ABS,

Even Aston Martin was initially reluctant to introduce a V8 Vantage Volante, as it could not guarantee that the hood would stay in place over 130mph. By this time, attempts to visually update the car for the eighties were proving rather ungainly.
(Courtesy David Hodges Collection)

four wheel drive, or any of the other safety accoutrements of the time. 50 were produced.

The most exclusive version, however, was the V8 Vantage Zagato Volante of 1987-90. Only 39 of these convertible Zagatos were produced, most with smooth-covered radiator grilles and concealed headlights. Usually commanding price upon application when they appear on the second-hand market, these cars can make up to £100,000. The V8 is, however, an inherently strong and charismatic car in all its guises, and the depreciation of earlier models makes them temptingly affordable – if you can sustain their running costs.

The final flowering of the 'original' Aston Martin V8 was the 1986 Zagato-bodied version, good for over 180mph.

Lancia Flavia 2000 Coupé

FIAT's 1969 takeover of fellow Italian marque Lancia provoked outrage amongst the cognoscenti, especially when it became known that Lancia, rather than using its unique recipe of bespoke front-wheel drive transmissions, and innovative, powerful engines, would use FIAT's homogenous, mass-produced take on front-wheel drive, and other hallmarks of platform-sharing and badge-engineering. Still, at least FIAT's rescue attempt would not preclude the removal of a traditional Lancia GT coupé from the range.

The Flavia 2000 Coupé proved to the doubting Thomases that FIAT was more than adept at the task of running Lancia (its links with Ferrari allowed for the later development of the legendary Stratos after all). The front-wheel drive set-up on the Flavia range provided sharp turn-in whilst liberating space inside through lack of an intrusive driveshaft. The race-inspired gearbox maintained some semblance of weight distribution, however. The action of the gearbox was satisfyingly slick, and the lack of oversteer made for a relaxing driving experience, concentrated on the sharp cornering and neatly responsive engine. No automatics were available (not unusual for an Italian

GT – Italian cars are so frequently rewarding of the keen driver), so sporting intent remained.

The engine was a two-litre flat four developed by Lancia and FIAT as an expansion of the previous, slightly underpowered 1.8, to keep the sporting character intact whilst providing a reliable and serviceable unit, a task it handled adeptly. The cylinder layout, coupled with its Italian predilection for revving, endowed the Flavia with an entertaining exhaust note.

Styling was the work of Pininfarina, which was clearly changing with the times. Rather than the voluptuous silhouettes and billowing curves found on previous Pininfarina classics, particularly Ferraris, the Flavia 2000 Coupé took a leaf out of comparative modernist Bertone's book. The Flavia featured crisp, straight lines, sharply shaped windows and a modern, clean front end featuring a simple grille and four headlights. Hints of Ferrari were still present though, with the 365GT 2+2-inspired chrome bumpers with inset lights, and the neat rear end with its low, unobtrusive oval light clusters and angled boot lid like the 330GTC's. Overall, the image was one of relaxed European sophistication, rather than American aggression, or the increasingly brutal and technical-looking British take on modernism.

Perhaps the Lancia Flavia 2000 Coupé will not go down as one of history's greatest GT cars, but its layout and style made it

SPECIFICATION
CYLINDERS = 4
CAPACITY (LITRES) = 2.0
POWER = 131BHP
TOP SPEED = 115MPH
TRANSMISSION = 4-SPEED MANUAL
DESIGN = PININFARINA
BUILT = 1969-74

The original Flavia 1.8 Coupé, current 1962-68.
(Courtesy David Hodges Collection)

highly influential in terms of the European car industry in the 1970s. Its looks were drawn upon strongly by Audi for its 100 series and by Ford for the Capri, and later Giorgetto Giugiaro for his Volkswagen Golf and Scirocco, and before long, many manufacturers were looking towards the square-jawed, flat-sided fastback shape to affect an air of grand touring aspiration into their ranges, even if the mechanicals did not back it up (in the case of cars such as the VW Polo Coupé, and FIAT's own 128 3P).

But of course, the Flavia's mechanicals did back up the image, and it was far more than just the style that Lancia's emulators borrowed from the Flavia. Since Lancia's introduction of front-wheel drive and sweet, rev-biased engines on the small Fulvia range, nearly every European sports coupé was drawn towards this layout, previously declared unsporting for so many years.

Rust, and a relatively short production life (five years) has meant the Flavia 2000 Coupé has been unfairly forgotten, especially considering its influence on the rest of Europe, but this trend-setter now exudes enigmatic, continental cool, and at around £5000 for a good one – if you can find one – it must surely be irresistible.

Marcos Mantis

There is a jocular understanding amongst the architectural community that the British could not convincingly work with modernism, and produced a variation called 'brutalism' instead. Countries such as France, Spain and Germany embraced modernism's experiments with bold

SPECIFICATION
CYLINDERS = 6
CAPACITY (LITRES) = 2.5
POWER = 150BHP
TOP SPEED = 120MPH
TRANSMISSION = 4-SPEED MANUAL OVERDRIVE
DESIGN = DENNIS ADAMS, MARCOS IN-HOUSE
BUILT = 1970-71
INNOVATION: THE FIRST KIT-BUILT GT CAR

colours, geometry and proportions with a sense of perspective and care, whilst the British used the wrong materials and designs that merely assaulted aesthetic sensibilities, with forbidding slabs of concrete, awkward proportions and lurid choices of colour, British brutalism not only found its way onto buildings and civil engineering, but also onto its cars. Some of the ugliest attempts at automotive futurism have been British – one only has to compare the British Austin Princess and Allegro with the comparable French Citroën CX and GS to see that, whilst European modernism was harmoniously evolutionary, British brutalism was violently reactionary.

Into the midst of this modernist frenzy, in 1970, rolled the Marcos Mantis. All the raw ingredients were present – a lusty, powerful and reliable fuel-injected Triumph straight-six engine, a luxuriously trimmed interior, independent front suspension revised from the Triumph GT6, smooth ride qualities, a rust-free fibreglass body and comfortable room for four. It was, in concept, a shrunken Lamborghini Jarama or similar, its only real rivals being the stricken Gilbern Invader and the pricey Reliant Scimitar GTE.

However, its two 'problems' as such – in fact two of the things that make this innovator so significant – were products of its ferocious Britishness: its kit-build construction, and its quirky, one might say brutalist, styling.

Kit cars are as central to British motoring culture as hot rods are to Americans and sophistication and suspension technology is to the French. British roads dictate that a British sports car's forte must be its handling. Also, fuel availability and taxation means that huge engines and massive weight are not welcome attributes to most owners. As a result, the majority of British sports car companies began by building fibreglass-bodied 'specials', utilising the reliable parts from mundane saloon cars, but improving the suspension and chassis so the car could corner more effectively and win races on Britain's tight, twisting

The Marcos Mantis might have looked odd, such was the Marcos lore, but there was no denying that it was anything other than futuristic. (Courtesy John Webster)

circuits. Lotus started this way, as did TVR, Ginetta, GTM and, of course, Marcos.

Marcos cars had always been unconventional kit-built sporting machines – some early cars had plywood monocoque construction – but the Mantis was a bold experiment for the British kit car scene – a GT car that was fast, refined, accommodating and luxurious, yet retained all the attributes expected of a British sports car – useable performance, ease of maintenance, and of course, excellent handling.

Part of the Mantis' problem lay in its styling. Rather than being a concoction of attractive curves like Marcos' sports car line-up, the Mantis featured a rubber-clad shovel nose, bug-eyed square headlights, ridged vents on the bonnet, a huge, oddly-shaped glasshouse out of proportion with the rest of the body, and body lines that didn't so much 'flow' as 'ripple'. Some pundits suggested that the car resembled rashers of bacon laid on top of each other. One thing was certain – it was well and truly modern, but in the sense of being a reaction against the traditional, rather than, say, the Italian school of modernism championed by the likes of Bertone, which worked with a mixture of all that modern technology could offer and sheer unconventionality.

All this was rather unfortunate, though, as it represented a new era for both the world of kit cars and the world of GTs. It proved that a GT could be truly capable, yet be built by an enthusiast on their own premises. It also proved that a kit car could be bestowed with the refinement and usability of a production car if built properly. Unfortunately, it sank as a result of its typically British take on radicalism – kit cars and modernism.

Firstly, the kit car market didn't take to it. Perhaps kit builders merely appreciated the rawness of more typical sports cars, especially from Marcos, which sold hundreds of its other models. It was also very expensive for a kit, especially in the post-purchase tax era of VAT, where there were no longer any financial advantages to buying a component car as opposed to a fully-built one.

The interior was perhaps more appealing, being modernist and uncluttered, and as unconventional as its bodywork.
(Courtesy John Webster)

Secondly, the mainstream market didn't take to it at all. Even though there were official Marcos 'build agents' who would build a customer's Marcos for them, few people outside of the kit car world knew about it. As a result, not only did the Mantis only survive one year in production, with just 39 examples completed, but Marcos suffered too, and ended up having to cut back all its production, surviving for the next ten years only producing the Mini-Marcos MkIV, a Mini-based, competition-orientated kit car, a world away from GTs like the Mantis.

The Mantis was ultimately a typically British failure – rooted in garden-shed enthusiasm placing engineering first, questionable looks second; a dearth of publicity, marketing strategy and aesthetic appeal made it impossible to sell. If only it had been differently designed (designer Dennis Adams insists even today that the Mantis looked nothing like he had originally intended), then perhaps it might have turned the fortunes of Marcos around. However, the fact that it didn't explains why Marcos has not attempted anything remotely similar since.

If you find the styling attractive, and can track down one of the 39, you will find yourself behind the wheel of one of the British motor industry's greatest missed opportunities. It still retains the qualities that promised so much back in 1970, and is still a capable, if thoroughly unconventional, Grand Tourer.

A Triumph-based kit car taking on Aston Martin? It might have been a commercial failure but the Mantis was a fine Grand Tourer with room for four. (Courtesy John Webster)

Citroën SM

If the Marcos Mantis sums up all the most British things about a car in a modernist GT, then the Citroën SM encapsulates all the best French automotive thinking in one package to produce a GT equally fantastic and unconventional, and then to add Italian supercar thrust courtesy of the French firm's acquisition of Maserati.

Citroën was already well known for its DS saloon. One of the automotive world's most enduring icons, the DS incorporated many technologies that, even today, the world has yet to come to terms with, yet alone try to replicate in anything other than the latest Citroën saloons. Amongst the DS's refinements were self-levelling hydropneumatic gas/liquid suspension, hydraulic parking brakes, pneumatic gearchange circuit, headlights that turned with the front wheels, and a single-spoke steering wheel that enabled the instruments to be visible for more of the time than a multiple-spoked affair which would obscure them. Front-wheel drive was another Citroën trademark, as was an aerodynamic body design that solved problems with wind resistance that even Ford struggled to rectify with its 1982 Sierra saloon.

SPECIFICATION
CYLINDERS = V6
CAPACITY (LITRES) = 2.7-3.0
POWER = 170-180BHP
TOP SPEED = 140MPH
TRANSMISSION = 5-SPEED MANUAL/3-SPEED AUTOMATIC
DESIGN = ROBERT OPRON, CITROËN IN-HOUSE
BUILT = 1970-75
INNOVATION: THE APPLIANCE OF ALL OF CITROËN'S TECHNOLOGY TO A GT

The DS featured all the groundwork for a great and boldly individual Grand Tourer, but it did lag behind in the engine department. The DS still used the big, long-stoke 'four' that started life in the 1936 Light 15 Traction Avant. Then the opportunity arose for Citroën to purchase Maserati – Citroën technology eventually found its way onto the Ghibli's successor the Khamsin, and later, the Merak.

The technology was refined, and the time was ripe, to release a proper Citroën GT car. Citroën commissioned a 90-degree version of the fine Giulio Alfieri-designed Maserati V6 for the new car, fitting it into a version of the DS chassis reconfigured for rallying to provide optimum handling, with the most advanced DS23 5-speed gearbox mounted ahead of it. Robert Opron, student of DS designer Flaminio Bertoni, styled a sleek, space-age coupé body for it, and it was another design classic. The low swage lines and full-width glass at the front was pure science fiction. If the DS had resembled a 1950s Dan Dare rocket ship, the SM was a flying saucer from the pages of Asimov. It was practical too, with as much seating space as a DS, and a rear hatch. There was even a four-door saloon, named 'Opera' and convertible version, 'Mylord', offered by French coachbuilder Chapron, of which sixteen and six were built respectively.

It added even more technology too, especially in the area of lighting. The SM featured six headlights – fixed main beams, the second pair were self-levelling and pointed up and down hills, and the inner pair were the same as those on the DS – they turned with the steering. The glass flaring across the front also enclosed the numberplate.

Driving an SM was quite unlike any other GT car on the road, then or now. The hydraulically assisted steering was as direct and sharp as an unassisted sports car's, yet smoother, completely insulated and feather-light, lessening its level of assistance as the car was driven faster. With an hydraulic clutch system, gearchanges were smooth too, if disconcerting for more traditional, controlling drivers, while its vice-like brakes, controlled by a floor-mounted button, could catch out the unwary with their sudden application. The ride was absolutely unrivalled, and the interior, with its sweeping plastic moulding and oval gauges, made the driver feel like they were piloting something otherworldly.

The car sold well initially, especially as the 2.7-litre 'injection electronique' V6 neatly fitted below the high French tax banding that came in at 2.8 litres. However, when the fuel crisis struck in 1973, and the French government acted punitively, this advantage disappeared overnight.

The fuel crisis placed Citroën in a difficult situation: the car

The beautifully unconventional SM, with a Maserati engine, front-wheel drive, hydropneumatic suspension circuit, and directional, self-levelling headlights. Few other GTs could claim to boast such levels of technology as the SM. (Courtesy David Hodges Collection)

was too thirsty to sell to its previous clientele, but perhaps not exclusive enough to move into the upper bracket dominated by Ferrari, Aston Martin, and, ironically, Maserati.

Driven into the hands of Peugoet, struggling to develop the new GS and CX saloons, and faced with an almost nonexistent UK market (mainly because the SM was left-hand drive only), in 1975 Citroën made one last stab at GT success with a 3-litre triple-Weber carburettor version of the Alfieri V6 from the Maserati Merak 3000GT, aiming for the American market. Unfortunately, it failed, as Americans were discouraged by the SM's complexity, unconventionality, and past reputation (long since solved) for unreliability, even though it was given a conventional automatic gearbox, and shared many design concepts with America's own Oldsmobile Toronado.

The last SM was built in 1975. Since then, it has become a greatly sought after classic GT car. The engineering still complicates restoration and ownership to some extent, but if you have fallen in love with the SM, none of this will matter. A true landmark GT car.

The SM in profile for a typical early-seventies publicity shot. Robert Opron's lines were American designer Art Blakeslee's first port of call when he penned the 1989 Citroën XM saloon. (Courtesy David Hodges Collection)

129

Triumph Stag

Convertibles have deliberately been avoided in this book, mainly because a car without a roof will never have the same refinement as the same car with one, and also because the majority of touring convertibles were roofless versions of GT coupés anyway, and so have been included alongside their coupé sisters.

However, the Triumph Stag of 1970 offered a convertible with the manners of a coupé. The neatly designed roof built on Triumph's 'Surrey Top' found on the TR4 sports car. The Stag featured a 'T-bar' roof, making for a safe roll bar (to appease the growing concerns of the American safety lobby surrounding convertibles), to which a solid, padded roof panel could be fixed, and a conventional soft-top roof pulled over the whole construction. Triumph also offered a sophisticated bolt-on hardtop with a heated rear windscreen that neatly integrated itself with the full-size, framed doors and the design feature of the stainless steel-clad roll bar. In short, with the roof up, the Stag was a proper four-seater GT coupé.

The styling was just about perfect too. Giovanni Michelotti designed the whole of Triumph's 1960s and 1970s ranges, and gave the Stag the same treatment as the 2000 and 2.5PI saloons. A tapered indentation front and rear held the lights, which seemed to fan outwards from a styling line running the length of the bodywork. Sweeping scalloping on the bonnet and boot completed the cohesiveness of the lines, all given an extra touch of glamour with a hint of American-style 'Coke bottle' hips.

SPECIFICATION

CYLINDERS = V8

CAPACITY (LITRES) = 3.0

POWER = 145BHP

TOP SPEED = 115MPH

TRANSMISSION = 4-SPEED MANUAL OVERDRIVE/3-SPEED AUTOMATIC

DESIGN = GIOVANNI MICHELOTTI, MICHELOTTI

BUILT = 1970-77

INNOVATION: COUPÉ REFINEMENT IN A CONVERTIBLE

The handling was typically sporting, as Triumph enthusiasts had come to expect from the likes of the TR, GT6 and Spitfire ranges, with a good chassis balance, rear-mounted gearbox and rear wheel drive. However, the Stag did not take long to gain a reputation for unreliability.

The main culprit was the engine. Due to corporate infighting at British Leyland, Triumph snubbed the chance to use the 3.5-litre Rover V8 and opted to build its own instead. To do so, it welded two Triumph Dolomite 1.5-litre slant-four blocks together on a common crankcase, also adapted from the four-cylinder Dolomite. The standard Dolomite radiator was also fitted. The result was chronic overheating, exacerbated by excessive crankshaft wear, as the crankcase was only designed to cope with the pressure of 1.5 litres and four cylinders. The radiator, being only really adequate for four cylinders, also contributed to overheating – it worked so hard that all it took was a small blockage to boil the water and overheat the engine too.

In the worst-case scenarios, the engine block cracked down the middle, where the welding was, and hot oil would ignite, causing extensive fires. Poor-quality Lucas electrics only made matters worse.

All this was immensely unfortunate as, other than this, the Stag was a great GT car. The small V8 produced adequate performance yet returned upwards of 20mpg, the interior was well finished, the bodywork was of good quality, and although Triumph looked into the possibility of a hatch-backed full-time coupé version, it was deemed unnecessary, due to the adaptability of the roof. Even so, the car's engineering shortcomings and compromises ensured an early retirement without much in the way of development. Production ceased in 1977.

Today, the Stag's problems have been overcome, sometimes by fitting different engines, (usually the 2.5-litre fuel injected straight-six from the PI saloon, or the 3.5 V8 from Rover that Triumph turned down), sometimes by fitting bigger radiators, stronger crankshafts and casings, and changing the oil at 3000-mile intervals. Either way, most Stags are now reliable GT cars, and prices have been rising steadily throughout the past decade. At long last, the Triumph Stag is delivering on what it promised so tantalisingly back in 1970 – GT adaptability in a convertible.

The Triumph Stag in a marvellously evocative 1970 publicity shot. The versatility of the adaptable roof is clear – it could function as a coupé and support skis, but also be completely removed, and still have the roll-over protection afforded by the stainless steel T-bar. (Courtesy David Hodges Collection)

Today's new era of folding-roof convertibles approach GT comfort, but the way the roof occupies boot space when folded compromises it. Perhaps sometimes, the simpler solutions really are the best after all.

FIAT 130 Coupé

When production of the Ferrari-engined FIAT Dino series approached an end, FIAT saw so reason why its name should not live on in the annals of European grand touring. Despite its ownership of Lancia, FIAT pursued production of the blocky and conventional 2.8-litre 130 luxury saloon, aimed squarely at competing with the BMW 2800 in all aspects. Pininfarina's styling mimicked many BMW cues, from the quadruple headlights, rakish overhangs and sharp lines all round. Unfortunately, it lacked a sense of Italian identity, and it was obvious that it was, in many ways, an object lesson in plagiarism gone wrong. The ultimate effect was one of blandness.

SPECIFICATION
CYLINDERS = V6
CAPACITY (LITRES) = 3.2
POWER = 165BHP
TOP SPEED = 115-118MPH
TRANSMISSION = 5-SPEED MANUAL/3-SPEED AUTOMATIC
DESIGN = PININFARINA
BUILT = 1971-77

The GT car launched alongside was, however, a completely different story. Seeking to capitalise on Bertone's styling of the previous Dino coupé, Pininfarina's 130 Coupé featured a low, wide, brooding front end dominated by narrow, squinting, oblong headlights, looking like an update of Bertone's Dino. The rest of the car was similarly long, low and severe in a wonderfully glassy way characteristic of so much European design of the late 1960s and early 1970s.

What pleased most, though, were the proportions. No one part of the car dominated or outweighed another, and the design was completely devoid of finicky details, fussy patterns or quickly dating fads. Pininfarina would go on to replicate many of the styling features on the Rolls-Royce Camargue of 1975, although that car's weight and sheer ostentation in some ways upset the neat balance seen on the 130 Coupé.

Mechanically, FIAT competed in-house with the outgoing Dino. Utilising many of the Dino's independent suspension components for similar ride and handling, and coupling it all to a unique 3.2-litre version of FIAT's V6 bored out solely for the 130 Coupé, top speed was nowhere near the Dino's 130mph, but it more than made up for it with road-burning torque. Though it revved well, sustained high-speed cruising was the 130 Coupé's forte.

To make the most of the power, keen drivers selected the excellent FIAT five-speed manual gearbox, which allowed the car to get close to 120mph. In reality, though, this market was dominated by buyers of automatics who frequently opted for the rather restrictive Borg-Warner three-speed unit. This strangled the rev-happy FIAT V6 in a way that did not affect the more torque-biased rival BMW straight-six.

This was just one way the market essentially mistreated this fine Italian GT. It was simply too radical for what was, by now, essentially a conservative sector. The FIAT badge, despite

Pininfarina's design for the FIAT 130 Coupé possessed a severe elegance that has been sadly dismissed since as boring. Its glassy execution and perfect proportions have rarely been bettered. (Courtesy David Hodges Collection)

A brochure image from the time plays on the 130 Coupé's subtle, sober good looks. (Courtesy Peter Jones)

its vague Ferrari associations, meant nothing to serial buyers of BMWs. Comparatively, between 1971 and 1977, BMW sold 21,371 of its CS coupés; FIAT only managed to shift 4491 130 Coupés. FIAT used its corporate power to ultimately replace it with the more prestigious Lancia Gamma in 1977, coinciding with the 130's ultimate demise.

Unfortunately image prevails and the 130 Coupé remains rather unknown. Its proportions are lost on the devotees of fashion who see its neatly understated looks as plain, and its typically '70s concoction of veneer and velour inside does not help. The FIAT reputation for extensive rusting was not lost on these cars either, so few remain. Those that do, however, represent a superb choice of classic Grand Tourer for connoisseurs of Italian modernist style and thoroughbred road manners. If you want one, patience and mechanical sympathy in abundance, will ultimately be rewarded with ambience and ability.

Bitter CD

Concept cars are the most attractive aspect of the industry for the car enthusiast with an eye for design. Unfettered by safety regulations or the financial implications of volume-building, a car designer can let his or her imagination flow when presented with the challenge of a concept, and can think aloud regardless of the marque's resources.

Rarely do concept cars make production, and it is more often the mundane saloons, hatches and off-roaders that do – cars designed with a strongly commercial aspect in mind. For a dramatic concept GT car to emerge virtually unchanged and built in volume for public consumption is decidedly unusual. Alfa Romeo's Brera is a recent example, and its celebrated status reflects the rarity of this occurrence.

Opel was to dispose of its GT concept, the CD, after its show appearances in the 1969-70 season. Simply an exercise in what the Opel design team was capable of, the big V8 GT with lines that aped the Ferrari 365 GTC/4 languished, without a future, at Opel's headquarters. Opel dealer, parts manufacturer and aftermarket options specialist Erich Bitter had other ideas.

Bitter had his eye on getting the CD into production whether Opel had plans for it or not. He managed to purchase the dramatic fastback coupé concept from Opel's design department and, after some rationalisation (using as many parts from Opel's Diplomat saloon range as possible, most significantly), made a conscious effort to put it into production.

Lacking his own factory, Bitter commissioned the Bauer coachbuilders of Stuttgart to manufacture the car bearing his name alongside BMW convertible conversions, bestowing

the CD with superb build quality. The American-designed V8 flung the light and aerodynamic GT car to nearly 130mph. Its displacement, identical to that of Aston Martin's V8, gave it similar low-down torque characteristics to the DBS V8, making them as fast as each other in day-to-day use as well. The car only came as an automatic though, inhibiting its potential to truly be an Aston Martin beater.

It might as well have been an Aston Martin rival considering the comparable cost. Erich Bitter's aftermarket sales background made tailoring a Bitter CD to one's own requirements more straightforward than with many other more exclusive marques with more history. 45 colours were available, along with a choice of materials as well as colours for the upholstery, dashboard finishes and driver options. Access to all of Opel's parts meant the saloon-derived systems were straightforward to use and service too. The Bitter was a buyer-friendly high-end GT.

The Bitter suffered, yet survived, the 1973-74 oil crisis, largely due to its wealthy clientele and Erich Bitter's small-scale operation, involvement with Bauer and other, more lucrative assets. However, where other GT builders like Aston Martin and Ferrari had the capital to update their cars, Bitter did not. The CD continued in production until 1979, still with a dinosaur of a V8 engine, 230bhp, 129mph and no manual gearbox option. Manacled to Opel's output, Bitter had to wait until the 1978 release of the Diplomat's replacement, the Senator, to begin work on a new GT more in keeping with the times.

Today, the Bitter CD makes for an interesting and highly affordable alternative to a Ferrari 365GTC/4, having similar styling with the slash-like rear windows, dramatic fastback and blade-like profile. However, with automatic transmission and Opel underpinnings, the driving experience is not quite so exotic. Still, the transmission and big, simple V8 are reliable and receptive to alternative fuel technologies, certainly making this big hatchback more practical than the Ferrari. The price, of course, represents not only the Bitter's affordability – if you can find one of the 390 constructed – but also its relative obscurity and massive depreciation. With the exception of the eccentric Bristol, it was the last of the small European companies sporting big American V8s for their exotic-rivalling power. It was also,

SPECIFICATION
CYLINDERS = V8
CAPACITY (LITRES) = 5.3
POWER = 230BHP
TOP SPEED = 129MPH
TRANSMISSION = 3-SPEED AUTOMATIC
DESIGN = OPEL
BUILT = 1971-79

Erich Bitter's CD, originally destined to be an Opel, was the last of the pre-oil crisis, American V8-engined GTs. It clearly took inspiration from the Ferrari 365GTC/4 in its styling. (Courtesy David Hodges Collection)

along with Bristol, one of the only ones to survive the fuel crisis by staying small, and therefore provides a fitting conclusion to our look at the pre-crisis GT form, a breed that would soon change forever.

1973 – the end of an era

The big GT cars of the fifties, sixties and early seventies were, despite our perspective on them today, highly advanced machines. Harnessing the affordable power of a big V8 or V12 engine merely extended the window of opportunity for builders of the grand touring breed to develop away from the larger manufacturers without worrying about sufficient reserves of power. The Jensen FF, for example, with its four-wheel drive and antilock brakes, proves that power was never an issue for Jensen.

However, Jensen (despite two abortive attempts at rebirth) no longer exists today, and the FF's technological successor, the Audi Quattro of 1981, serves to remind us of the radical changes forced upon the whole car industry by the oil crisis.

During the sixties, the prevailing peacetime, a general lack of environmental concerns and American prosperity allowed for cheap fuel and few, if any, qualms connected to its profligate use. For many, such as Iso and Jensen, it seemed that this era had no end, and they embraced it for all its worth, dependant on this 'feelgood factor'.

In 1973, however, the Arab-Israeli war broke out in the Middle East, and Europe and America were forced to come to terms with the finite nature of oil. The war abruptly ceased (albeit temporarily) the regular and sizeable availability of oil, prompting the West to rapidly reel in its vast consumption. A state of emergency soon followed. Recovery from the recession-induced industrial crisis in Britain was hampered further by fuel shortages and 50mph motorway speed limits. American car manufacturers soon realised the shortcomings of its thirsty cars and started importing economy-minded runabouts, or building their own characterless iterations.

This sense of panic was soon followed by a wave of environmentalism and concerns about the impact of 'the car'. Cars had to become more economical and cleaner in terms of emissions, but

Opposite: Manufacturers like Aston Martin were left in limbo by the fuel crisis. Unable to effectively downsize, they passed into receivership, and prices, aimed at an exclusive clientele and driven by rampant inflation, ballooned. (Courtesy David Hodges Collection)

Following the fuel crisis, many GT manufacturers followed the Alfa Romeo recipe – small-to-medium sized engine, low weight, and low-drag aerodynamics. (Courtesy David Hodges Collection)

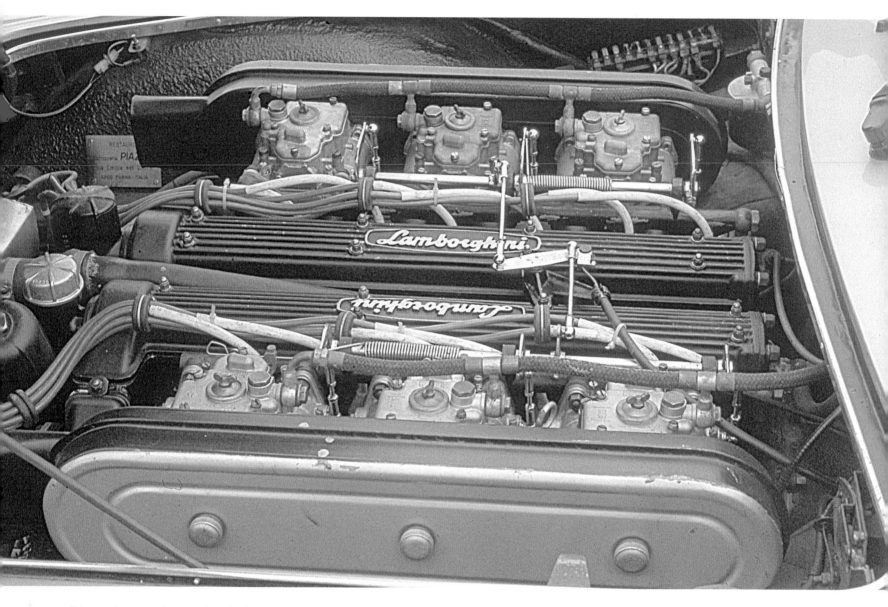

Big engines and towering fuel consumption were relatively unimportant issues in the sixties. However, better fuel economy dictated automotive engineering in the seventies. Even Lamborghini prepared small V8s of 2 to 3.5 litres for its seventies GT, the mid-engined two-plus-two Uracco.
(Courtesy David Hodges Collection)

safety also became an issue of importance – crash and roll protection legislation from America made the hedonistic sixties suddenly seem a lifetime away. 1973 certainly was the end of an era.

Was it the death knell for classic GTs? Compare that Jensen FF with that Audi Quattro again. The Audi is lighter, it corners more sharply, the engine delivers the power of the Jensen's without the thirst, it has its roots in top-level motorsport and it is easier to live with, brimming with charisma. It is no less the GT the Jensen was. 1973 might have been the end of one great era, but its unfortunate demise heralded another just as significant in terms of automotive and cultural advancement.

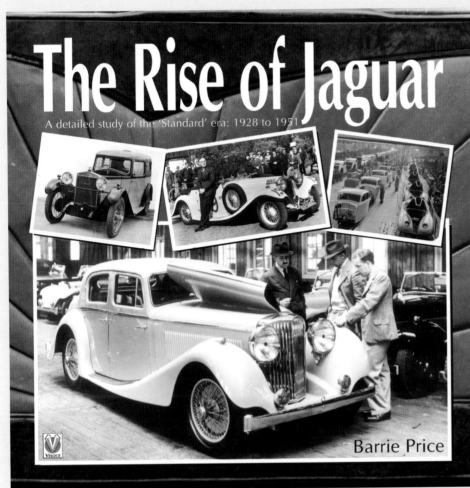

The Rise of Jaguar
Barrie Price
£37.50*

ISBN: 978-1-904788-27-0

A serious in-depth study of the growth of SS Cars Limited during the world's worst economic depression; the relationship with the Standard Motor Company upon which success was based, together with a detailed technical survey covering the progression of design from 1928 to 1950.
Many hitherto unknown facts disclosed; copiously illustrated with contemporary photographs.

"This is a great and entertaining addition to the Jaguar story." *Jaguar Magazine*

"[The author's] authoritative study will appeal to all who have ever owned an early Jaguar, or who wanted to." *The Oldie*

Jaguar E-type V12 5.3 litre & Jaguar E-type 3.8 & 4.2 litre – the Essential Buyer's Guides
Peter Crespin
£9.99* each

Buying a car is an expensive business and mistakes can prove costly financially and in time, effort and stress. Wouldn't it be great if you could take an expert with you? With the aid of these books' step-by-step guidance from a marque specialist, you can!

These pocket-sized books steer buyers past the dazzling exterior to examine systematically, section by section, cars they are considering. Picture-packed to help orientate even newcomers and ensure they buy the best car for their budget.

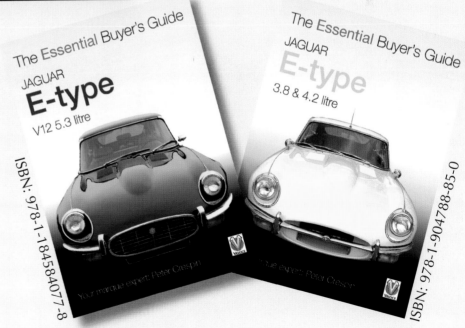

Note: P&P extra. Prices subject to change. Visit our website, or email sales@veloce.co.uk for details.

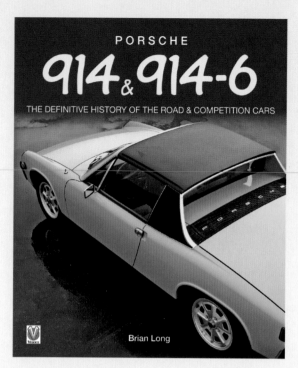

Porsche 914 & 914-6 – the definitive history of the road & competition cars
Brian Long
£29.99* (hardback)/£19.99* (softback)

ISBN: 978-1-84584-014-3/ISBN: 978-1-84584-030-3

Perceived as a reasonably priced entry level model for Porsche, the 914's early history was blighted by political problems with VW's new management. However, by the end of production, almost 119,000 examples had been sold. This book records the full international story of the mid-engined 914, from concept through to the final production car, illustrated throughout with contemporary material. Today, the 914 is an affordable and practical classic.

Ford GT – Then, and Now
Adrian Streather
£40.00*

ISBN: 978-1-84584-054-9

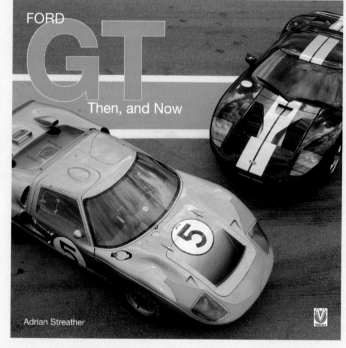

Starting in 1956 when Ford officially entered motor racing, this book takes the reader on a journey of how and why things happened the way they did. Who were the personalities behind the all the different Ford GT development programs, old and new. Driver's have been interviewed, never before seen historical and new photographic records have been included, and some of the old myths and legends have been revisited.

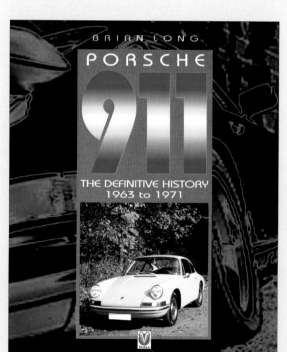

Porsche 911 – the definitive history 1963 to 1971
Brian Long
£35.00*

ISBN: 978-1-903706-28-2

The first in a series of five books which chronicle in definitive depth the history of the evergreen 911, from the earliest design studies to the water-cooled cars of today. This volume covers original design, the 901 prototype, the early 911s (including 912s), and the 2.2 litre cars.

*Note: P&P extra. Prices subject to change. Visit our website, or email sales@veloce.co.uk for details.

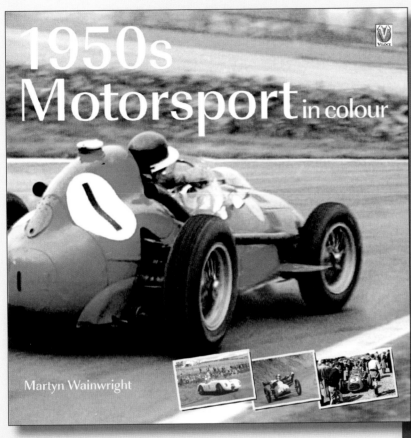

1950s Motorsport in colour
Martin Wainwright
£29.99*

ISBN: 978-1-904788-15-7

A unique collection of rare original colour photographs of Grand Prix and sports cars, taken between 1954 and 1959 at races and hillclimbs in England & Ireland. This book is an absolute must for 'Revivalists' and all lovers of classic motorsport.

"An amazing archive of colour racing photos." *Classic & Sports Car*

"This book is a wonderful evocation of the way things used to be." *The Telegraph*

Motor Racing – Reflections of a Lost Era
Anthony Carter
£39.99*

ISBN: 978-1-904788-10-2

A defining era in motorsport documented in words and intimate photographs, both black and white and colour, from the mid-1950s through the 1960s, when motor racing was still accessible to all, and the 1970s when overt sponsorship and television changed the sport forever.

"It draws you in so much that the smells and sounds of the period paddock seem to seep out of its pages." *Startline*

"Before I had finished, I knew this was a book I was going to keep for ever." *CarKeys*

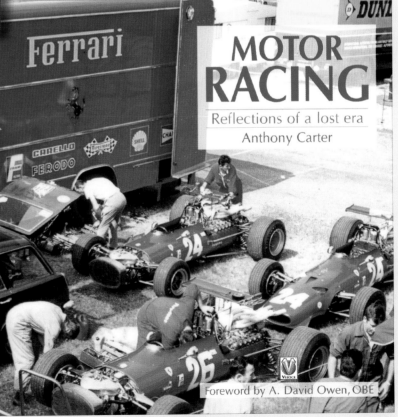

Note: P&P extra. Prices subject to change. Visit our website, or email sales@veloce.co.uk for details.

Index

AAC Avanti 82, 84
Abbot (coachbuilders) 20
AC 428 38, 78, 104, *104*, 105, *105*
AC Ace 37
AC Aceca 37, *37*
AC Cobra 23, 37-38, 104-105, 121
AC Greyhound 37, *38*, 104
Adams, Dennis 126-127
Alfa Romeo 26, 93, 117
Alfa Romeo 101-series (engine) 32
Alfa Romeo 105-series (engine) 67
Alfa Romeo 2600 Berlina 53-54
Alfa Romeo 2600 Spider 53-54, *136*
Alfa Romeo 2600 Sprint 53, *53*, 62
Alfa Romeo 2600 SZ 54
Alfa Romeo 6C 53
Alfa Romeo 8C 2900B 30
Alfa Romeo Brera 93
Alfa Romeo Disco Volante 30
Alfa Romeo Duetto Spider 67
Alfa Romeo Freccia d'Oro 30
Alfa Romeo Giulia GT 32, *44*
Alfa Romeo Giulia GTA 67-68, *68*
Alfa Romeo Giulia GTC 67-68, *68*
Alfa Romeo Giulia GTV *67*, 100, 106
Alfa Romeo Giulia Sovralimentato 68
Alfa Romeo Giulia Spider 32
Alfa Romeo Giulia Sprint GT 67-68
Alfa Romeo Giulia SS 10, 30, *30-32*, 32
Alfa Romeo Giulia SZ *11*, 32, *32*
Alfa Romeo Giulia TI Berlina 67, *67*
Alfa Romeo Giulietta 53
Alfa Romeo Giulietta Berlina 30
Alfa Romeo Giulietta Spider 30
Alfa Romeo Giulietta Sprint Berlinetta 30
Alfa Romeo Giulietta Sprint Speciale 32
Alfa Romeo Giulietta Sprint Veloce 30
Alfa Romeo Giulietta SS 30, *31*, 32,
   67-68
Alfa Romeo Giulietta SZ 30
Alfa Romeo GT Junior 67-68
Alfa Romeo GTV 68
Alfa Romeo Junior Z 68
Alfa Romeo Villa d'Este 30
Alfieri, Giulio 35, 76, 128-129
Altman, Nathan 82, 84
Alvis 15, 74, 91
Alvis Speed 25, 29

Alvis TC108G 29
Alvis TD21 28-29, *28-29*, 70
Alvis TE21 69, 69-70
Alvis TF21 69-70
Andress, Ursula 26
Appleyards (rally drivers) 20
Aston Martin 15, 18, 20, 24, 28, 35, 37,
   45, 66, 70, 76, 86, 96, 108, 117, 119,
   123, 129
Aston Martin AM Vantage 71, 73
Aston Martin DB1 18
Aston Martin DB2 7, 18, 33
Aston Martin DB2/4-series 6, 12, 18, 29,
   33-34, 38
Aston Martin DB2/4 Mk I *19*
Aston Martin DB2/4 Mk II 18
Aston Martin DB2/4 Mk III 18, 33
Aston Martin DB3S 18
Aston Martin DB4 10, 18, *33*, 35, 49, 51,
   65, 70, 76
Aston Martin DB4 GT 33-34
Aston Martin DB4 GT Zagato 34, *34*, 40,
   54
Aston Martin DB4 Vantage 33-34, 71
Aston Martin DB4 Vantage GT 34
Aston Martin DB5 34, 71-72, 76
Aston Martin DB6 71-72, *72*, 78
Aston Martin DBA Vantage (engine) 18
Aston Martin DBC Competition
   (engine) 18
Aston Martin DBR4 34
Aston Martin DBS 54, 71-73, *73*, 120
Aston Martin DBS V8 120, *120*, 134
Aston Martin DB 'Sotheby Special'
   120-121
Aston Martin DP114 71
Aston Martin DP212 34
Aston Martin Nimrod 122
Aston Martin V8 73, 120, *121*
Aston Martin V8 Vantage 120, 122, *122*,
   137
Aston Martin V8 Vantage Volante *123*
Aston Martin V8 Volante 120, 122, *122*
Aston Martin V8 Zagato 6, 120, 123, *123*
Aston Martin Volante 71
Audi 100 125
Audi 99
Audi Quattro 102, 136, 138

Austin 65
Austin A70 24
Austin Allegro 126
Austin DS7 (engine) 24
Austin Princess 126
Austin Seven 10
Austin Sheerline 24
Autodelta (tuners) 67
Avanti 44, 86
Avanti II 82

Baron, The 65
Bauer (coachbuilders) 134
Bentley 10, 22, 29, 51, 57, 70, 74
Bentley Continental *11*, 16-17, *17*, 18,
   23, 29, 55-56
Bentley Continental S2 16, *16*
Bentley MkVI 16, 22
Bentley S3 Coupé 55, *56*, 57
Bentley T1 Coupé 55
Bertone 26, 30, 32, 47, 53, 58-59, 67,
   85, 114, 124, 127, 132
Bertone BAT 30, 32
Bertone, Nuccio 47
Bertoni, Flaminio 128
Bianchi, Signor 33
Bitter CD 134, *135*
Bitter, Erich 134
Bizzarini, Giotto 58, 96
Blake, Stephen 84
Blakeslee, Art 129
Blatchley, John 16
Blow-Up 56
BMC 70
BMC P6BS 70
BMW 14, 54, 58, 75, 82, 97, 132, 134
BMW 2.5 CS 95
BMW 2000CS 93-94
BMW 2000ti 93-94
BMW 2002 94
BMW 2800 132
BMW 2800CS 94
BMW 3.0 CS 94, *94*
BMW 3.0 CSL 95, *95*
BMW 3200CS 26
BMW 503 26, *27*, 93
BMW 507 26, 93
BMW 5-Series 26

BMW 6-Series 26, 39, 84, 95
BMW 700 93
BMW 8-Series 26
BMW CS-series 93, *93*
BMW CSA 94
BMW CSI 94
BMW CSL 94
BMW Isetta 26, 58, 93
BMW M1 111
BMW Turbo Concept 111
Bond Equipe 6
Bond, James 16, 18, 45, 71
Borg-Warner (gearboxes) 81, 88, 132
Bracq, Paul 111
Bristol (engine) 37-38
Bristol 14, 24, 29, 65, 135
Bristol 400-series 16
Bristol 401 14, *14-15*
Bristol 404 15, *15*
Bristol 405 15, 62
Bristol 406 15, 62
Bristol 406Z 15
Bristol 407 *61*, 61-62
Bristol 408 61-62
Bristol 409 61-62
Bristol 410 61-62
Bristol 411 61-62, *61-63*
British Leyland 130
Brosnan, Pierce 71
Brown, David 34, 72, 121
Buckley, Martin 24
Bugatti Royale 7
Buick Riviera 74-75, *74-75*, 82, 92, 102,
   108
Bunting, Jim 84

Cadillac 10, 74, 111
Cadillac Eldorado 7, 75, 92
Cadillac Eldorado Biarritz 16
Cadillac Series 62 Coupé 16
Campbell, Malcolm 29
Chapman, Colin 32
Chevrolet 58-59, 86
Chevrolet Camaro 6, 72, 82
Chevrolet Corvette 58, 82, 84-86
Chrysler 14, 22-23, 51, 61, 65
Chrysler Torqueflite (gearbox) 51, 62,
   65, 102

Italicised page entries indicate photographs.

Citroën 44, 78-81
Citroën CX 126, 129
Citroën DS 49, 80, 82, 128
Citroën GS 126, 129
Citroën Light 15 Traction-Avant 128
Citroën SM 51, 92, 128-129, *129*
Citroën SM Mylord 128
Citroën SM Opera 128
Clapton, Eric 30
Coca-Cola 82
Columbo, Giocchino 41
Company Developments 121
Concorde 66, 114
Connery, Sean 34, 71, 106
Cord L29 Sportsman 91
Crook, Tony 15, 62

Daimler 87
Daimler Majestic 12
Daimler SP250 'Dart' 87
Daimler SX250 87
Dallara, Giampaolo 96
Dalton, Timothy 122
Daninos, Jean 22, 51
Datsun 240Z 54
Dean, James 82
DeDion (suspension) 12, 99
DeTomaso 23
DeTomaso Deauville 58
DeTomaso Longchamps 104
DeTomaso Pantera 23, 89, 96
DeTomaso, Alejandro 81
Dino (engine) 47
Dino 206GT 47, 90
Dodge Challenger R/T 62
Dodge Charger 440 R/T 66
Draco, Marc-Ange 56
Dunlop Maxaret (brakes) 102
Duran Duran 122

Eastleigh Airport, Southampton 86
Enever, Sydney 62
Eon Productions 106
European Touring Car Championships
   (ETCC) 93, 95

Facel Vega 14, 58, 61
Facel Vega Facel II 51, *52*
Facel Vega Facel III 51
Facel Vega Facellia 51
Facel Vega FVS 22, *22*, 51
Facel Vega HK500 23, *23*, 51, 58
Fangio, Juan Manuel 12, 35, 79
Feeley, Frank 18, 33
Ferguson Formula 102
Ferrari 12, 26, 34-35, 49-51, 60, 62, 71,
   74-75, 78-79, 96-97, 114, 124, 129,
   132-133
Ferrari 250GT California 41, *41*, 108
Ferrari 250 Tour de France 41
Ferrari 250GTB Lusso 41-42, *42*, 89
Ferrari 250GTE 10, *41*, 41-42, 47, 58, 89

Ferrari 250GTO 41-42, 89
Ferrari 250LM 41
Ferrari 250PF Coupé/Cabriolet 41
Ferrari 250SWB 34, 41-42
Ferrari 250 Testa Rossa 41
Ferrari 275GTB/4 80, 89-90
Ferrari 330 (engine) 42, 96
Ferrari 330 America 41-42
Ferrari 330GT 2+2 89
Ferrari 330GTC 89-90, *90*, 106, 124
Ferrari 365 California Spider 89, 108
Ferrari 365GT 2+2 6, 90, *108-109*,
   108-110, 124
Ferrari 365GT4 110
Ferrari 365GTB/4 'Daytona' 6, 44, 47,
   49, 58-59, 90, 92, 109-110, 122
Ferrari 365GTC 89-90
Ferrari 365GTC/4 6, 92, 109-110, *110*,
   121, 134
Ferrari 500 Superfast 98, 108
Ferrari 612 Scaglietti 10, 41
Ferrari Maranello 89
Ferrari Superamerica 108
Ferrari Testarossa 89
Ferrari, Alfredino 47
Ferrari, Enzo 30, 32, 47, 49, 89
Ferzetti, Gabriele 56
FIAT 39
FIAT 124 47
FIAT 130 Coupé 132-133, *133*
FIAT 20v Turbo Coupé 42, *48*
FIAT 2300S 47, *48*, 54
FIAT Dino Coupé 47, *48*, 132
FIAT Dino 2000 Spider 47
FIAT Mephistopheles 47
Fioravanti, Leonardo 108
Firestone (tyres) 108
Fittipaldi, Emerson 59
Fleming, Ian 16
Ford 59, 82, 88, 104-107, 118, 121
Ford 302 (engine) 50
Ford Capri 67, 100, 125
Ford 'Cleveland' (engine) 58-59
Ford 'Cologne' (engine) 119
Ford Comete 22
Ford Cortina 100
Ford 'Essex' (engine) 88, 100, 117, 119
Ford Galaxie 104-105
Ford Granada 119
Ford Mustang 50, 82, 115
Ford Shelby Mustang GT500 58
Ford Popular 24
Ford Sierra 128
Ford Taunus 100
Ford Zephyr 87-88
Ford Zetec (engine) 107
Formenti, Federico 33
Formula 1 12, 33, 35, 79, 102, 106
Friese, Bernard 100
Frua, Pietro 45, 76, 78 104

Gandini, Marcello 114

General Motors 74-75, 82, 91
Ghia 47, 58, 79
Gilbern Genie 100-101
Gilbern Invader 100-101, *101*, 118, 126
Ginetta 127
Girling (brakes) 127
Giugiaro, Giorgetto 58-59, 67, 78-79,
   85, 125
GM Hydramatic (gearbox) 92
GM 'Rocket' (engine) 75, 92
Godfather, The 30
Goertz, Count Albrecht 26, 93
Gold Leaf cigarettes 106
Goldeneye 71
Goldfinger 18, 71
Gordon GT 86
Gordon-Keeble GK1 44, *44*, *85-86*,
   85-87, 100
Gordon, Irv 46
Gordon, John 85-86
Gordon-Keeble 23
Graber 29
Group B rallying 102
GT racing 6, 34, 41, 71, 89
GTM 127

Harrison, George 89
Hawthorne, Mike 12
Heinkel 58
Helena Rubenstein Cosmetics 87
Hemming, David 56
Hickman, Ron 106
Hoffmeister, Wilhelm 58, 93-94
Hot Rod Garage 84
Hutton, Barbara 89

Indianapolis 500 80
Invicta Black Prince 10
Iran, Shah of 79
Iso 23, 44, 61, 75, 96, 122, 136
Iso Fidia 58-59
Iso Grifo 58-59, *59*
Iso Grifo 90 60
Iso Lele 58-60, *60*, 116
Iso Rivolta 58, *58*
Iso Varedo 60
Isothermos 58
Italian Job, The 47

Jaeger 35
Jaguar 24, 26, 45, 66, 70, 78, 87
Jaguar MkI 21
Jaguar MkII 3.8 21
Jaguar SS100 20
Jaguar XJS 50, 84
Jaguar XK (engine) 18, 22, 29, 49, 50
Jaguar XK120 6, 10, 20-21
Jaguar XK120C/'C-type' 20-21, 49
Jaguar XK140 6, 20-21, *21*
Jaguar XK140 'B-type' 21
Jaguar XK150 21, *21*, 29
Jaguar XK150S 21

Jaguar XKD/'D-type' 21, 49
Jaguar XKE/'E-type' 7, 18, 21, 49-51,
   49-50, 65, 71, 86-87, 99
James Young (coachbuilders) 55, 57
Jano, Vittorio 12
Jeep 96
Jensen 23, 86, 122, 136
Jensen 541 24, *25*, 30, 32, 64
Jensen 541S 45
Jensen CV8 64-66, *64-65*, 86
Jensen FF 66, 102-103, *103*, 136, 138
Jensen GT 66
Jensen Interceptor 64, 66, *66*, 100, 102,
   117, 119,
Jensen P66 66
Jensen S-Type 24
Jensen SV8 66
Judas Priest 122

Karen, Tom 87, 117, 120
Keeble, Jim 85-86
Kelly, Michael 84

Lagonda 18, 24, 72-73, 122
Lagonda LB6 (engine) 18
Lamborghini 350 GT 96-97
Lamborghini 350 GTV 96
Lamborghini 400GT 7, *7*, 96-97, *96*
Lamborghini 96
Lamborghini Countach 60, 96, 116
Lamborghini Espada 8, *8*, *43*, 97,
   114-116, *114-115*, 138
Lamborghini, Ferrucio 71, 96
Lamborghini Islero 96-97, *97*
Lamborghini Jarama 60, 114-116,
   116, 126
Lamborghini Marzal 114
Lamborghini Miura 44, 60, 79, 96-97,
   114-116
Lamborghini Urraco 116
Lancia 10, 18, 26, 66, 76, 82, 132
Lancia Aurelia B10 saloon 12
Lancia Aurelia B20 GT 6-7, 12, *13*
Lancia Flaminia 86
Lancia Flaminia Coupé 39
Lancia Flaminia GT 39, *40*
Lancia Flaminia Spider *39*
Lancia Flaminia SSZ 40, *40*
Lancia Flavia 1.8 Coupé *124*
Lancia Flavia 2000 Coupé 124-125, *125*
Lancia Flavia 40
Lancia Florida 39
Lancia Fulvia 125
Lancia Gamma 133
Lancia Stratos 124
Land-Rover 96
Le Mans 16, 18, 33, 108
Learjet 105
Lennon, John 59
Lincoln 92, 111
Lincoln Continental 75
Llantwit Major (factory) 100

Loewy, Raymond 82, 84
Lotus 10, 24, 32, 44, 47, 55, 109, 127
Lotus 'Big Valve' (engine) 107
Lotus Elan +2 106-107, *107*
Lotus Elan 45
Lotus Elan S4 106
Lotus Elan Sprint 107
Lotus Elite (Climax) 106
Lotus Elite (500) 107
Lotus Esprit 60
Lotus Europa Special 107
Lotus MkIX 32
Lotus Seven S3 106
Lotus Seven SS 107
Lotus Twin Cam (engine) 106
LPG (fuel) 23
Lucas (electrics) 130
Lucky Strike cigarettes 82
Lyons, William 20, 49

Maggoria 76
Man Who Haunted Himself, The 97
Maranello (factory) 41, *41*
Marazzi (coachbuilders) 97
Marcos 24, 127
Marcos Mantis 126-127, *126-127*
Marek, Tadek 34, 73, 120
Marles (steering racks) 62
Maserati 10, 12, 18, 41, 60, 97, 128-129
Maserati 250F 35
Maserati 3200GT 78
Maserati 3500 GT IS 76
Maserati 3500GT Spider *36*
Maserati 3500 GTI 35
Maserati 3500GT 35, 40, 76, 79
Maserati 450S 35
Maserati 5000GT 35, 78-79
Maserati A6GS 35
Maserati Bora 81
Maserati Due Posti 76
Maserati Ghibli 35, 78-80, 128
Maserati Ghibli SS 58
Maserati Indy 79-81, *80-81*
Maserati Khamsin 35, 81, 128
Maserati Kyalami 81, 104
Maserati Merak 81, 128-129
Maserati Mexico 78-81, *79*
Maserati Mistral 76, 78, *78*, 80, 104-105
Maserati Quattroporte 58, 78-79
Maserati Sebring 35, 76-78, *77*
Mazda 110S Cosmo 98-99, *98-99*
Mazda 128B Cosmo 99
Mazda 44
Mazda RX-7 99
Mazda RX-8 99
McCartney, Paul 71
McQueen, Steve 56
Mercedes-Benz 51, 69, 122
Mercedes-Benz 190 'Ponton' 111
Mercedes-Benz 220/250 saloon 111

Mercedes-Benz 220/300 saloon 111
Mercedes-Benz 300SL 26, 79
Mercedes-Benz 600 111
Mercedes-Benz CE 111, *112*
Mercedes-Benz S-Class 111
Mercedes-Benz SE 111, *113*
MG B 68, 100
MG Midget 100
MG T-Series 10, 20
Michelin (tyres) 108
Michelotti, Giovanni 26, 35, 76, 79, 85,
   93-94, 130
Middlebridge 119
Miller 91
Mini-Marcos MkIV 127
Mitchell, Bill 74, 91
Monaco Grand Prix 114
Montiverdi 23
Moore, Roger 45, 97, 120
Moss (gearboxes) 20
Mulliner Park Ward (coachbuilders) 55
Mulliner, HJ (coachbuilders) 16, 18
Mundy, Harry 50

Nardi 12, 35
Nardi, Enrico 32
Nash 16
Neale, Eric 24, 64
Neil, Christopher 107
Newman, Leo 82, 84
NSU 98-99
NSU Ro80 98

Ogle Design 87-88, 117, 120-121
Ogle Triplex GTS 88
Ogle, David 87
Oldsmobile 44, 92
Oldsmobile Toronado 91-92, *91-92*,
102,
   129
On Her Majesty's Secret Service 56, 72
Opel 134
Opel Diplomat 134
Opel Senator 103, 134
Opron, Robert 128

Packard Hawk 82
Pagani Zonda 96
Pagani, Horacio 96
Panhard 24CT 10
Panhard CD 10
Park Ward (coachbuilders) 29, 69
Parkes, Mike 89
Peel, Emma 45
Peerless 85
Persuaders, The 120
Peugeot 47
Pininfarina 12, 39, 41-42, 89, 124, 132
Pininfarina, Battista 39
Pininfarina, Sergio 41, 47, 108

Plant, Robert 75
Pont-a-mousson (gearboxes) 51
Pontiac Firebird 82
Pontiac Trans-Am 82
Porsche 47, 97
Porsche 911 12, 95
Porter, Boris 87
Presley, Elvis 26
Pressed Steel (coachbuilders) 55
Prince Charles, HRH 122
Prince Philip, HRH 88, 117
Princess Anne, HRH 118-119

Ranier, Prince of Monaco 12
Reliant 88
Reliant Regal 87, 118
Reliant Rialto 118
Reliant Robin 87, 118
Reliant Sabre Six 87
Reliant Scimitar 87-88, *87-88*, 117
Reliant Scimitar GTC 117, 119
Reliant Scimitar GTE 88, 117-119,
   117-118, 126
Reliant Scimitar SS1 119
Renault 66
Rivolta, Piero 58, 60
Rivolta, Renzo 58
Rolls-Royce 16, 24, 29
Rolls-Royce Camargue 57, 132
Rolls-Royce Corniche 55-57, *57*
Rolls-Royce Silver Cloud 17
Rolls-Royce Silver Shadow 57
Rolls Royce Silver Shadow Coupé 55
Rosengart Supertrahuit 10
Rover 29, 70, 93
Rover P5 70
Rover V8 (engine) 130
Rudd, Ken 37

Saint, The 45
Salisbury (differentials) 96
Sayer, Malcolm 49
Scaglione, Franco 30
Scheel (racing seats) 94
Sellers, Peter 56, 62
Shelby, Carroll 37, 121
Shinoda, Larry 114
Simca 66
Simmons, Jean 14
Sinatra, Frank 66
Smart, Billy 120
Smith, Giles 107
Sotheby cigarettes 121
Spada, Ercole 33, 39, 40, 54, 120
Springfield, Dusty 75
Spyder Engineering 107
Standard Vanguard 16
Studebaker Avanti 82-85, *83-84*
Studebaker Starlight Commander 82
Subaru 45

Superleggera 10, 18, 33, 96

Templar, Simon 45
Thomas Crown Affair, The 56
Thunderball 16, 71
Tickford 18
Tjaarda, Tom 89
Touring of Milano 10, 33, 35, 67, 71, 96
Towns, William 71-72, 120-121
Toyota 2000GT 106
Triplex glass 88, 121
Triumph 26, 79, 126
Triumph 2.5 PI 130
Triumph Dolomite 130
Triumph GT6 6, 126, 130
Triumph Spitfire 130
Triumph Stag 119, 130-131, *131*
Triumph TR4 130
Trojan 58
Turner, Edward 87
TVR 10, 24, 127

Vallone, Raf 47
Vanden Plas Princess 70
Vauxhall Cresta 16
Vignale 12, 36, 64, 66, 79, 80, 102
Vignale, Alfredo 64, 76, 102
Volkswagen 35
Volkswagen Golf 125
Volkswagen Polo Coupé 125
Volkswagen Scirocco 6, 125
Volvo 117
Volvo 1800E 45
Volvo 1800ES 45
Volvo 1800S 45, *46*
Volvo 480ES 45, 119
Volvo B18 'Amazon' 45
Volvo P1800 6, 45, 51, 54
Volvo P1900 45

Wankel (engines) 98-99
Wansborough, George 86
Watson, Willie 18
Weber (carburettors) 42
Wilks, Maurice 96
Williams, Frank 60
Williams, RS 34
Willis, Bruce 82
Willowbrooks (coachbuilders) 29
Wolfrace (wheels) 119
Woolworth's 89

You Only Live Twice 106

Zagato 12, 14-15, 30, 32-34, 39-40, 54,
   67, 71, 120, 122
Zagato Mini 40
Zagato Zimp 40
Zagato, Gianni 14-15
ZF (gearboxes/steering racks) 70, 81, 96